The Book of Abraham

By George Reynolds

ISBN: 978-1-63118-540-3

Mormon History Series

Other Books in this Series and Related Titles

Pearl of Great Price by Joseph Smith (978-1-63118-539-7)

The Testament of Abraham by Abraham (978-1-63118-441-3)

The Book of Parables by Enoch (978-1-63118-429-1)

The Secrets of Enoch by Enoch (978-1-63118-449-9)

American Indian Freemasonry by A C Parker (978-1-63118-460-4)

Lost Chapters of the Book of Daniel and Related Writings (978-1-63118-417-8)

The Book of the Watchers by Enoch (978-1-63118-416-1)

Book of Dreams by Enoch (978-1-63118-437-6)

The Hymns of Hermes by G. R. S. Mead (978-1-63118-405-5)

The Book of Astronomical Secrets by Enoch (978-1-63118-443-7)

The Two Great Pillars of Boaz and Jachin by A Mackey &c (978-1-63118-433-8)

The Regius Poem or Halliwell Manuscript by King Solomon (978-1-63118-447-5)

The Lost Keys of Freemasonry or The Secret of Hiram Abiff (978-1-63118-427-7)

Brothers & Builders by Joseph Fort Newton (978-1-63118-506-9)

Symbolism and Discourses on the Entered Apprentice, Fellowcraft and Master Mason Blue Lodge Degrees by various (978-1-63118-413-0)

Freemasonry in the Medieval or Middle Ages by various (978-1-63118-450-5)

Freemasonry, Mithraism and the Ancient Mysteries by various (978-1-63118-407-9)

The Ceremony of Initiation: Analysis & Commentary (978-1-63118-473-4)

The Symbols and Legends of Masonry by C H Vail (978-1-63118-504-5)

The Janeites, The Man Who Would Be King and Other Stories of Freemasonry by Rudyard Kipling (978-1-63118-480-2)

Audio Versions are also available on Audible, Amazon and Apple

Other Books in this Series and Related Titles

Rosicrucian Rules, Secret Signs, Codes and Symbols by various (978-1-63118-488-8)

History and Teachings of the Rosicrucians by W W Westcott &c (978-1-63118-487-1)

Freemasonry and the Egyptian Mysteries by C. W. Leadbeater (978-1-63118-456-7)

The Sepher Yetzirah and the Qabalah by M P Hall (978-1-63118-481-9)

The Psalms of Solomon by King Solomon (978-1-63118-439-0)

The Legend of the Holy Grail and its Connection with Templars and Freemasons by A E Waite (978-1-63118-462-8)

Masonic and Rosicrucian History by M P Hall & H Voorhis (978-1-63118-486-4)

The Kabbalah of Masonry & Related Writings by E Levi &c (978-1-63118-453-6)

Some Deeper Aspects of Masonic Symbolism by A E Waite (978-1-63118-461-1)

Masonic Symbolism of King Solomon's Temple by A Mackey &c (978-1-63118-442-0)

The Old Past Master by Carl H Claudy (978-1-63118-464-2)

The Influence of Pythagoras on Freemasonry and Other Essays (978-1-63118-404-8)

The Mysteries of Freemasonry & the Druids by various (978-1-63118-444-4)

Masonic Symbolism of the Apron & the Altar by various (978-1-63118-428-4)

The Book of Wisdom of Solomon by King Solomon (978-1-63118-502-1)

Masonic Symbolism of Easter and the Christ in Masonry (978-1-63118-434-5)

The Odes of Solomon by King Solomon (978-1-63118-503-8)

Ancient Mysteries and Secret Societies by M P Hall (978-1-63118-410-9)

The Golden Verses of Pythagoras: Five Translations (978-1-63118-479-6)

Freemasonry & Catholicism by Max Heindel (978-1-63118-508-3)

A Few Masonic Sermons by A. C. Ward &c (978-1-63118-435-2)

Audio versions are also available on Audible, Amazon and Apple

Table of Contents

THE BOOK OF ABRAHAM

ITS AUTHENTICITY ESTABLISHED AS A DIVINE AND ANCIENT RECORD

WITH COPIOUS REFERENCES TO ANCIENT AND MODERN AUTHORITIES

BY
ELDER GEORGE REYNOLDS

CHAPTER 1

INTRODUCTORY.--THE DISCOVERY AND SUBSEQUENT HISTORY OF THE MUMMIES.--TRANSLATION OF THE PAPYRUS BY THE PROPHET JOSEPH SMITH.

THE late republication of the pearl of great price has drawn renewed attention to the Book of Abraham, which forms a portion of its contents. And as but very little has ever been said by the Elders of the Church in advocacy of its claims as an inspired record, written by one prophet of God in the infancy of the earth's history, and translated by another prophet of the Most High in the dispensation of the fulness of times, we think that a few chapters written to prove its genuineness and divine origin, will not be without value to the Latter-day Saints, and to the world at large. For while the people of God have said or written little in its defense, there have been those opposed to the revelations of God in these days, who have vigorously attacked it, who have styled its language "gibberish," and classed it among the "pious frauds" that have so often disgraced the history of religion, Christian and heathen. We hold, and we have confidence that we can prove, by history, science, and in various other ways, that the Book of Abraham is exactly what it claims to be, and that it was translated by the wisdom and power of God for the benefit of the human family, by the Prophet Joseph Smith.

Before entering into the discussion of its contents, we deem it advisable to say a few words with regard to the manner in which it fell into the possession of our martyred Prophet. The account he gives in his history of this incident, is to be found under date of December 30, 1835, (Vol. XV. Millennial Star,) from which we condense: He states that the records from which the Book of Abraham was translated were found in one of the catacombs, near the city of Thebes, in Egypt, in the year 1831, by a French traveler named Antonio Sebolo, who had received permission from Mehemet Ali, the then ruler of Egypt, to open it. After vast labor, an entrance was effected on the 7th of July, 1831, and several hundred mummies discovered therein, in various stages of decomposition. M. Sebolo obtained eleven of the best preserved mummies and started with them for Paris, the capital of France. On the way he was taken sick, and after an illness of ten days, died at Trieste. In his will he left these valued remains of ancient Egyptian art to his nephew, Mr. M. H. Chandler, and after various vicissitudes they came into this latter gentleman's possession in April, 1833. He proceeded to make a living by their exhibition, and traveled about the country for that purpose, reaching Kirtland July 3d, 1835. In the meantime he had opened the coffins and found "that in connection with two of the bodies was something rolled up with the same kind of linen, saturated with the same bitumen, which, when examined, proved to be two rolls of papyrus." "Two or three other small pieces of papyrus, with astronomical calculations, epitaphs, etc., were found with others of the mummies." In Joseph's history is the following account of Mr. C's visit to Kirtland.

"On the 3d of July Michael H. Chandler came to Kirtland to exhibit some Egyptian mummies. There were four human figures, together with some two or more rolls of papyrus covered with hieroglyphic figures and devices. As Mr. Chandler had been told I could translate them, he brought me some of the characters, and I gave him the interpretation, and like a gentleman he gave me the following certificate:

' KIRKLAND, July 6, 1835.

'This is to make known to all who may be desirous, concerning the knowledge of Mr. Joseph Smith, jun., in deciphering the ancient Egyptian hieroglyphic characters in my possession, which I have, in many eminent cities, showed to the most learned; and, from the information that I could ever learn, or meet with, I find that of Mr. Joseph Smith, jun., to correspond in the most minute matters.

'MICHAEL H. CHANDLER,

' Traveling with, and proprietor of Egyptian mummies.' "[1]

The Prophet, a few days later, writes: "Soon after this some of the Saints in Kirtland purchased the mummies and the papyrus, and I, with W. W. Phelps and O. Cowdery as scribes, commenced the translation of some of the characters or hieroglyphics, and much to our joy found that one of the rolls contained the writings of Abraham, another the writings of Joseph of Egypt, etc., a more full account of which will appear in their place as I proceed to examine and unfold them. Truly we can say the Lord is beginning to reveal the abundance of peace and truth."

From this time it appears from the history that Joseph set himself diligently to work to translate the records, as often as his other important duties permitted. Under date of October 1st, he records in his journal: "This afternoon I labored on the Egyptian alphabet, in company with Brothers O. Cowdery and W. W. Phelps, and during the research, the principles of astronomy as understood by Father Abraham and the ancients, unfolded to our understandings." It is desirable that these dates and facts should be remembered, as they have an important bearing on our future inquiries. Under date of October 7th, November 24th, and in other places, he refers to his labors in translating the papyrus. He also makes frequent reference to showing his friends these records, and of explaining to them their contents, not only to those in the Church, but to numbers who were not members. We will simply cite one instance. "December 16th, 1835. Elders McLellin, B. Young, and J. Carter called and paid me a visit, with which I was much gratified. I exhibited and explained the Egyptian records to them, and explained many things concerning the dealings of God with the ancients, and the formation of the planetary system."[2]

The next thing we deem in order is to give the Prophet's description of the appearance of the papyrus, which description, we may remark in

---

[1] History of Joseph Smith, Millennial Star, Vol. XV, page 285.
[2] History of Joseph Smith, Millennial Star, Vol. XV, page 519.

passing, is identical with that of President John Taylor, who frequently saw them when in Brother Joseph's possession. The latter writes:[3]

"The record of Abraham and Joseph, found with the mummies, is beautifully written on papyrus, with black, and a small part with red, ink or paint, in perfect preservation. The characters are such as you find upon the coffins of mummies, hieroglyphics, etc., with many characters or letters like the present (though probably not quite so square) form of Hebrew, without points."

Before proceeding further, it will doubtless be desirable to give a slight sketch of the contents of those portions of the Book of Abraham already translated and published. It opens with a short account of his early life at the home of his father in Ur of Chaldea, of the persecutions he suffered for righteousness' sake from his idolatrous kindred, and of the causes that led him to leave Chaldea for Canaan. It gives, at greater length than does the Bible, the covenants made with him by the Almighty, and affords some exceedingly interesting details with regard to the history of the priesthood in that early day. Further on an account of Abraham's visit to Egypt is given, and the revelations of God to him, with regard to the order of the planetary worlds, the condition of the spirits of mankind in their pre-existent state, and a history of the creation of this earth are laid before the reader in plain and simple, but inspired and soul inspiring language. No short synopsis can give any idea of the beauty, grandeur and value of the truths made manifest by the Most High to his friend and servant, Abraham; truths which the world, to-day, in part ignores and partly comprehends. We suggest to our readers the study of this important, though brief fragment, feeling assured that they will arise from its perusal with a more exalted and more comprehensive realization of the power, the glory and the love of God, than the study of any uninspired treatise could ever give, no matter how beautiful its language, or how sublime its thoughts.

It is our intention, as we pass along, to take up the various subjects treated in the Book of Abraham, and demonstrate the exact truthfulness of the record, by the writings of historians, ancient and modern, by the discoveries of archaeologists, Egyptiologists, astronomers and other scientists, and prove, we believe, beyond the possibility of successful contradiction, that no element of fraud enters into its composition. So

---

[3] Ibid, Vol. XV, page 550.

remarkable have been the confirmatory evidences that we have met in our investigations into this subject, that we are of the opinion that there is not a book in existence whose genuineness can be more easily proven than can that of the record of the Father of the Faithful. Being thus fully assured, we shall lay the forthcoming chapters before our readers with the joyful assurance that they will add to the already incontrovertible testimonies that Joseph Smith was a prophet, seer and revelator, and servant of the Most High God.

We make this last statement advisedly, because it must be evident to all who seriously consider the matter, that if the Book of Abraham as given to us by Joseph Smith be true, it must have been translated by a greater than human power. We well know that so far as the wisdom of this world is concerned, Joseph Smith was an unlearned man, unskilled in the higher branches of science, with little other knowledge than that which heaven conferred, but had he been a scientist of the highest order the production of the Book of Abraham would be but little less remarkable, as many of the truths taught therein (as we shall presently see) are in advance of the times, and were as unknown to the sage as to the simpleton in the year that the papyrus was translated, and indeed for many years afterwards. Consequently, human learning and human wisdom could not give them to the world. By some other power, which we claim was divine, they must have been revealed and made manifest.

CHAPTER 2

ABRAHAM'S EARLY LIFE IN UR.-- HUMAN SACRIFICES.-- CAUSES WHICH LED ABRAHAM TO LEAVE CHALDEA.-- CONFIRMATORY TESTIMONY OF JOSHUA, JOSEPHUS, THE BOOK OF JUDITH, ETC.

OF the early history of Abraham's life very little is said in the Book of Genesis. The mere fact is stated that his father's dwelling place was in Ur of the Chaldees, where the patriarch married his kinswoman Sarai, where also his brother Haran died.[4] After these events, it is recorded, Terah, his father, took a portion of the family and removed to Haran, where he dwelt until the day of his death, but the causes that led to his removal are not given. The next chapter opens with the command of God to Abraham, "Get thee out of thy country, and from thy kindred," etc., but the reasons why God gave him that command are not mentioned, not even hinted at. The Book of Abraham supplies many interesting details on this point not to be found in the history given by Moses, and that the details thus supplied are consistent with the condition of life in Egypt and Chaldea at that time, and in many respects corroborated by the writings and sayings of men living in later ages, it now becomes our business to prove.

Abraham states, in the second paragraph, into which his book has been divided, that his fathers had "turned from their righteousness and from the holy commandments which the Lord their God had given unto them, unto the worship of the gods of the heathens," and that "they turned their hearts to the sacrifice of the heathen in offering up their children unto their dumb idols." In the next paragraph it is written, "Now at this time it was the custom of the priest of Pharaoh, the king of Egypt, to offer up upon the altar which had been built in the land of Chaldea, for the offering unto these strange gods, men, women and children." A little further on Abraham writes, "And it came to pass that the priests laid violence upon me that they might slay me also. * * * And as they lifted up their hands upon me that they might offer me up and take away my life, behold, I lifted up my voice unto the Lord my God, and the Lord hearkened and heard, and he filled me with a vision of the Almighty, and

[4] Genesis, chap. xi.

the angel of his presence stood by me, and immediately unloosed my bands, and his voice was unto me, Abraham! Abraham! behold, my name is Jehovah, and I have heard thee, and I have come down to deliver thee, and to take thee away from thy father's house, and from all thy kinsfolk, into a strange land that thou knowest not of, and this because they have turned their hearts away from me, to worship the god of Elkenah, and the god of Lebnah, and the god of Mahmack-rah, and the god of Korash, and the god of Pharaoh, king of Egypt; therefore I am come down to visit them, and to destroy him who hath lifted up his hand against thee, Abraham, my son, to take away thy life."

To substantiate the truthfulness of the above statements, we ought to be able to bring testimony in favor of four points:

1st, That human sacrifice was practiced in Egypt and adjacent countries in Abraham's day.

2d, That Abraham's fathers were idolaters.

3d, That he was persecuted by his fellow countrymen because he opposed their idolatry.

4th, That God commanded Abraham to leave Chaldea, because his father's house had turned their hearts away from him to the worship of strange gods.

If the above points can be proven by other testimony than that of the Book of Abraham, we think we have strong evidence that the record is historically correct. Admit this, and we have taken a very decided step towards acknowledging the authenticity of the entire work. For it is very improbable, nay, almost absurd, to imagine that Joseph Smith, with his limited range of ancient historical knowledge, could have produced a work of this kind that would be historically correct. Had the work been a forgery, that is, had it originated with Joseph Smith, the probabilities are overwhelming that he would have made some egregious blunders, which could easily have been detected, and the whole affair, from beginning to end, proven a tissue of falsehoods.

Firstly, then, we have to show that human sacrifices were offered to the strange gods of the heathen in Abraham's day; more particularly in

Egypt, as it is represented that it was the priest of Pharaoh who officiated on the occasions mentioned by the patriarch.

To substantiate this point we shall make but one quotation, as its author mentions so many other historians, ancient and modern, as his authorities, that in quoting it we call upon them to become our witnesses also. It is taken from Dissertation II, Whiston's Josephus, and is as follows: "It is evident from Sanchoniatho, Manetho, Pausanias, Diodorus, Siculus, Philo, Plutarch and Porphyry, that such [human] sacrifices were frequent both in Phoenicia and Egypt, and that long before the days of Abraham, as Sir John Marsham and Bishop Cumberland have fully proved: nay, that in other places (though not in Egypt) this cruel practice continued long after Abraham."

We may here draw attention to the statement that this cruel practice did not continue in Egypt after Abraham's day, owing, we doubt not, as will hereafter be shown, to the great influence that that patriarch wielded in later life with Pharaoh and his subjects, in favor of a more perfect way of serving heaven.

Again, that Abraham's fathers were idolaters, though the book of Genesis carries no such inferences, as also that Abraham was commanded by Jehovah to leave his father's house because of this idolatry, is proven, we consider, by the following extracts. We will first turn to the Book of Judith, in the Apocrypha (chap, v, verses 6 to 9). It is there represented that when the invading hosts of the king of Nineveh were approaching the land of Israel, the commanding general made some inquiries with regard to the history of its people. Then Achior, the captain of all the sons of Ammon, in answer to his inquiries, replied: "This people are descended of the Chaldeans, and they sojourned heretofore in Mesopotamia, because they would not follow the gods of their fathers which were in the land of Chaldea. For they left the way of their ancestors, and worshiped the God of heaven, the God whom they knew, so they cast them out from the face of their gods, and they fled into Mesopotamia and sojourned there many days."

From the above it is very evident that the facts relating to the "call of Abraham" were not only well known to the Hebrews, but to the people of the surrounding nations also. As Achior was one in high authority among the sons of Ammou, his words under the peculiar circumstances in which they were uttered, would carry great weight, and if unauthorized would meet with severe criticism and probable contradiction.

But the question is forever set at rest by the words of a greater than Achior. Joshua, the valiant, God-fearing leader of Israel, shortly before his death, gathered the people together and rehearsed in their hearing the great things the Lord had beforetime done for them. It is written that at this time[5] "Joshua said unto all the people, Thus saith the Lord God of Israel, Your fathers dwelt on the other side of the flood in old time, even Terah, the father of Abraham, and the father of Nachor, and they served other Gods. And I took your father Abraham from the other-side of the flood and led him throughout all the land of Canaan, and multiplied his seed." And again,[6] "Now, therefore, fear the Lord, and serve him in sincerity and in truth, and put away the gods which your fathers served on the other side of the flood and in Egypt, and serve ye the Lord. And if it seem evil unto you to serve the Lord, choose ye this day whom ye will serve, whether the gods your fathers served that were on the other side of the flood, or the gods of the Amorites, in whose land ye dwell; but as for me and my house, we will serve the Lord." Further evidence than this we deem unnecessary, as here we have the end of all controversy, even the word of the Lord on the matter.

We cannot prove, directly from the writings of any authors at our disposal, that an attempt was made to take Abraham's life for righteousness' sake; but we can show from the "Antiquities" of Josephus that he was maltreated for that cause. This historian, after referring to the doctrines taught by Abraham, regarding God, writes, "for which doctrines, when the Chaldeans and other people of Mesopotamia raised a tumult against him, he thought fit to leave that country; and at the command and by the assistance of God, he came and lived in the land of Canaan."

---

[5] Joshua, chap, xxiv, v. 2, 3.
[6] Joshua, xxiv, v. 14, 15.

CHAPTER 3

ABRAHAM AS A PREACHER OF RIGHTEOUSNESS.--THE TESTIMONY OF PAUL.-- HIS MINISTRY IN UR AND HABAN.-- GOD'S COVENANT WITH HIM BASED ON THE GOSPEL.

PAUL, the Apostle, in his epistle to the Galatians, writes: "And the Scripture foreseeing that God would justify the heathen through faith, preached before the Gospel unto Abraham, saying, In thee shall all nations be blessed." The record of the covenant made by the Almighty contained in the Book of Genesis, conveys no intimation that the promise that in Abraham all the families of the earth should be blessed, was in any way connected with the preaching of the Gospel; we must, therefore, conclude that the Apostle quoted from some other authority, or that the Book of Genesis, as handed down to us in the Bible, has been mutilated or abridged. It is quite possible that both views are correct. Paul had unquestionably other sources of information with regard to God's dealings with the Father of the Faithful, than those possessed by modern Christendom; it is also exceedingly probable that the early Scriptures have not been handed down to us in their entirety. No matter, this does not affect the subject under consideration; the point to which we desire to draw attention is, that the Book of Abraham sustains the Apostle's statements that the covenant was based upon the preaching of the Gospel, whilst Paul's testimony, on the other hand, confirms the veracity of Abraham's record.

The covenant, as given by the latter, is as follows: "And the Lord appeared unto me, and said unto me, Arise, and take Lot with thee, for I have purposed to take thee away out of Haran, and to make of thee a minister to bear my name in a strange land, which I will give unto thy seed after thee for an everlasting possession when they hearken to my voice. For I am the Lord thy God; I dwell in heaven, the earth is my footstool; I stretch my hand over the sea, and it obeys my voice: I cause the wind and the fire to be my chariot; I say to the mountains, depart hence, and behold they are taken away by a whirlwind, in an instant, suddenly. My name is Jehovah, and I know the end from the beginning, therefore my hand shall be over thee, and I will make of thee a great nation, and I will bless thee above measure, and make thy name great among all nations, and thou shalt be a blessing unto thy seed after thee, that in their hands they shall bear this ministry and priesthood unto all nations, and I will bless them through thy name; for as many as receive this Gospel shall be called after thy name, and shall be accounted thy seed, and shall rise up and bless thee, as their father; and I will bless them that bless thee; and will curse them that curse thee; and in thee (that is, in thy priesthood) and thy seed (that is, thy priesthood), for I give unto thee a promise that this right shall continue in thee, and in thy seed after thee (that is to say, the literal seed or seed of the body) shall all the families of the earth be blessed, even with the blessings of the Gospel, which are the blessings of salvation, even of life eternal."

We would here ask, what salvation could be brought to the heathen, how could they be justified through faith by the preaching of the Gospel to Abraham, if power and authority were not given him to preach its glad tidings? And again, how could they be benefited thereby if he did not avail himself of the privilege thus given of becoming a preacher of righteousness to his fellow man? Furthermore, we ask, is it reasonable to suppose that he, who was to be father of that race in whom all the families of the earth were to be blessed by the preaching of God's word, would not himself be a type of what such messengers of salvation should be? Is it supposable he would hold his peace and leave the work of regeneration entirely to his posterity, when it was promised that through the eternal truths revealed to him all mankind should regain the presence of their God? We think not, and further, we imagine that his record would lack consistency if some reference was not made to his ministry and labors. And several such references we actually find more or less direct and conclusive with regard to his acts as a priest of the Most High. In fact, the whole of his writings are pervaded with this spirit, and are full of his anxieties to be a preacher of truth and righteousness. The opening paragraph of his book abounds with this feeling, indeed it contains nothing else; he writes, "finding there was greater happiness and peace and rest for me, I sought for the blessings of the fathers, and the right whereunto I should be ordained to administer the same, having been myself a follower of righteousness, desiring also to be one who possessed great knowledge, and to be a greater follower of righteousness, and to possess a greater knowledge, and to be a father of many nations, a prince of peace; and desiring to receive instructions, and to keep the commandments of God, I became a rightful heir,[7] a High Priest, holding the right belonging to the fathers, it was confirmed upon me from the fathers; * * * I sought for mine appointment unto the priesthood; according to the appointment of God unto the fathers concerning the seed." After the attempt of the priest of Pharaoh to take his life, the Almighty tells him, "Behold I will lead thee by the hand, and I will take thee to put upon thee my name, even the priesthood of thy father, and my power shall be over thee. As it was with Noah, so shall it be with thee, that through thy ministry my name shall be known in the earth for ever, for I am thy God." Still further on the Lord says: "I have purposed to take thee away out of Haran, and to make of thee a minister to bear my name in a strange land." Not only in Canaan was he to be a messenger of God's word, but the Almighty afterwards tells him, "I shew these things unto thee before ye go down into Egypt, that ye may declare all these words."

Thus we find that Abraham, having sought for the privilege of becoming a preacher of righteousness, in answer to his desire the priesthood was given to him with the command to magnify it. It is not probable that such a man would fail in the hour of action. The friend of God and Father of the Faithful was one "who knew no such word as fail," in carrying out heaven's commands. That he did proclaim the law of the Lord wherever he went, is evidenced by his statement that in his youthful home in Ur, his kinsfolk utterly refused to hearken to his voice. So earnest did he become in his advocacy of the truth, that his death was decided upon, even by his own father, and he did not flinch from the issue, but the angel of God rescued him from the sacrificial altar; his work was not yet done. In another place he states, "I took the souls that we had won in Haran, and came forth in the way of the land of Canaan." We shall presently discover, by outside testimony, that his ministrations were not alone confined to Ur and Haran.

We feel fully persuaded that Abraham was not only great in his unflinching integrity and his unswerving faith, but he was also great as a leader of men--he commanded his children and his household after him-- and as a preacher of the divine word. We hold this opinion from the fact that his power in these directions is frequently referred to by ancient writers, and because the effects of the preaching of God's holy word can

[7] Abraham, in another place, states that "the records of the fathers, even the patriarchs, concerning the right of priesthood, the Lord ray God preserved in my own hands." By this means, amongst others, he no doubt learned that he was "a rightful heir."

be traced in Gospel ideas mixed with the follies of heathenism in the mythology and religions of almost every leading nation of antiquity.

We have shown from the Book of Abraham, that in early life the patriarch desired to become a preacher of righteousness, that God conferred the priesthood upon him in answer to his desires, and commanded him to proclaim the truths He revealed, and furthermore, that Abraham joyously fulfilled His command. It is not to be supposed that strangers could tell the world much about Abraham's desires, or the Lord's covenants with him, but we can substantiate, from a multitude of sources, that as a preacher righteousness the patriarch has left his mark indelibly inscribed on the history of the world. That, indeed, as God promised so He has fulfilled, and has made Abraham's "name great among all nations," and has also brought to pass His gracious promise, "through thy (Abraham's) ministry my name shall be known in the earth forever."

To prove this will be our pleasure in succeeding chapters.

CHAPTER 4

ABRAHAM IN EGYPT.--CONFIRMATORY STATEMENTS OR JOSEPHUS, NICOLAUS OF DAMASCUS, AND OTHERS.--ABRAHAM'S INFLUENCE ON THE RELIGIONS OF EGYPT, PERSIA AND HINDOOSTAN.--TRACES OF GOSPEL TEACHING IN THE MYTHOLOGIES OF EGYPT, PERSIA, CHALDEA, GREECE AND ROME.--FIRST DEPARTURES FROM THE TRUE FAITH.--THE EGYPTIAN WORSHIP OF ADAM AND THE PATRIARCHS.--THE BOOK OF THE DEAD.

THE Book of Abraham states that God commanded the patriarch to show unto the Egyptians the things that He had revealed unto him. Josephus, in narrating this portion of Abraham's history--being only partially acquainted with the facts of the case from the authorities at his disposal--tell us that Abraham went down into Egypt to avoid the famine in Canaan, and to "become an auditor of their priests, and to know what they said concerning the gods; designing either to follow them if they had better notions than he, or to convert them into a better way if his own notions proved the truest."[8] After his arrival in Egypt, and the circumstances arising out of the attempt of Pharaoh to add Sarah to the number of his wives, the outcome of which placed the monarch under obligations to the patriarch, Josephus states that "Pharaoh gave Abraham leave to enter into conversation with the most learned among the Egyptians, from which conversation his virtue and his reputation became more conspicuous than they had been before. For whereas the Egyptians were formerly addicted to different customs, and despised one another's sacred and accustomed rites, and were very angry one with another on that account, Abraham conferred with each of them, and, confuting the reasonings they made use of, every one for his own practices, he demonstrated that such reasonings were vain and void of truth; whereupon he was admired by them in those conferences as a very wise man, and one of great sagacity, when he discoursed upon any subject he undertook; and this not only in understanding it, but in persuading other men also to assent to him."[9] In another place the Jewish historian states, "He (Abraham) was a person of great sagacity, both for understanding all things, and persuading his hearers, and not mistaken in his opinions; for

[8] Josephus, Antiquities, Book 1, chap. viii.

[9] Ibid, Book 1, chap. viii.

which reason he began to have higher notions of virtue than others had, and he determined to renew and to change the opinion all men happened then to have concerning God."[10]

So far as Josephus' testimony, confirmatory of this portion of the Book of Abraham, is concerned, we deem the above abundant. In later chapters we shall show the great political and religious changes that Abraham's visits to Egypt produced.

From Egypt we will turn to Persia, and from the writings of various modern authors adduce testimony to prove that Abraham's power as a religious teacher was felt, known and recognized in the faith and creed of that nation.

In the sacred book of the ancient Persians and modern Parsees-- the Zend Avista--"it is declared that the religion taught in it was received from Abraham; and according to Hyde, who supports his statements by quotations and references, this was believed by leading Arabian writers not only of Persian Magianism but of Indian Brahmanism." The same writer remarks: "The claims of Magianism to have been influenced by the revelations made to Abraham are far from being discountenanced by the laws of historical probability. For the war waged so successfully by Abraham in behalf of his kinsman, Lot, against the five kings, among whom was the king of Elam [i.e., Persia], is of itself a sufficient proof that the Father of the Faithful, Abraham, the Hebrew from Ur of the Chaldees, must have been as well known to the eastern kingdoms as Moses was in after times."[11]

It is generally admitted that in the days of Abraham the forefathers of the Persians and Brahmins were one people, inhabiting one region of country. It is supposed that the ancestors of the latter race moved to India from 1500 to 1300 years B. C. That these two races are of common descent is urged from the close relationship existing between the Sanskrit, the language of the Brahmins, and the Zend or Persian; it is also said that the "remarkable identity between the Brahminical and Persian mythologies indicates, unerringly, the original union of the two." It may also be noticed that Hitzig, in his "Geschichte dcs Volkes Israel," reasons from the identity of certain practices observed by Abraham and the

---

[10] Ibid, Book 1, chap. vii.

[11] Ethnic Inspiration, by Mr. Goodsir, pages 73 and 80.

patriarchs of Israel on the one hand, and by Brahminical Hindoos on the other, that a community of some kind once existed between these people.

The two nations being thus admitted, by authors of research, to have been one people in Abraham's time, it is supposable that the Brahmin as well as the Persian branch of the family would exhibit some traces of Abraham's ministry. On this point it has been written "Abraham's influence extended to Bactria, and the most complete proof at once of its spread, and the spread with it of the name and renown of Abraham, is contained in the language and name of the Brahminical Hindoos."[12]

"The name Brahma signifies he who multiplies; the name Abraham likewise means the father of a multitude. (Arabic, Rahama, a multitude. Genesis xxii, 5.) The wife of Brahma was named Savitree. The wife of Abraham was named Sarai or Sarah."[13]

Mr. Goodsir, remarking on this last extract, writes: "These coincidences appear to us to be well deserving of attention, though we are not aware that they have ever before been noticed. We leave them and the whole question of the identity of Brahma and Abraham to the judgment of our readers, merely observing, in conclusion, that having found Adam and Noah and Ham to have been the father-gods of Egyptian mythology, and Japhet the father-god of that of Greece, there is abundant analogy as well as probability in our inference that the father-god of the Indian superstition was Abraham."

Admitting the truth of the following extract from the writings of Nicolaus of Damascus, referred to by Josephus, it is very easy to understand when and how Abraham obtained his great influence in Persia; and we know of no conflicting testimony to render the statements unworthy of our consideration. He writes, in the fourth book of his history: "Abram reigned in Damascus, being a foreigner, who came with an army out of the land above Babylon, called the land of the Chaldees; but after a long time he got him up and removed from that country also, with his people, and went into the land then called the land of Canaan, but now the land of Judea. * * * Now the name of Abram is even still famous in the country of Damascus, and there is shewed a village named from him, the habitation of Abraham."

---

[12] Ibid.

[13] Osborn's "Religions of the World."

We now come to the consideration of the traces, ofttimes scarcely discernable, found in the pagan religions of the ancient nations of the eastern continent, of a time when the worship of the true God was taught and understood in their midst, for we fully believe that having made of one blood all the nations of the earth, "God guided and ruled over pagan nations in a manner the same in kind, though much modified in degree, as in the case of the chosen people; and for the same great final end." Let it not be supposed, in the following pages, that we desire to extenuate the sinfulness, or to palliate the foulness of idolatrous, cruel, unclean and licentious paganism in any of its branches. Our desire is to exalt the goodness of God, as well as to show that under all the vileness, the indecency, the lust and cruelty of many of the forms of ancient paganism, could be found a sub-stratum of pure revealed truth, testifying to us that at some period the fathers of these peoples held intercourse with the servants of the true God, but had fallen away from the principles of righteousness aforetime taught them, and after their own peculiar ways and to suit their own peculiar notions and desires, had heaped to themselves gods and demons, creeds and rites, ceremonies and mysteries, oracles and auguries, differing in different nations according to the force of circumstances and the direction given to them by master minds.

As a proof of the truth of our position, we have but to refer to the fact that it has been demonstrated that the further we go back through the centuries to the primeval days succeeding the dispersion of mankind at the Tower of Babel, the more frequent and more noticeable are the traces of pure religious truth found intermingled with the follies and vagueries of man-made religions. As an example of this, it is recounted by Levy, the Roman historian, that certain sacred books having been found at the burying place of Numa, the great religious legislator of early Rome, they were burned because they were not suited to the times in which they were discovered, when Rome had added scores of gods to its Pantheon, though they were considered suited to the early era in which they were written, when Numa forbade images and their worship as well as the offering of human sacrifices.

It is not difficult for those who believe in the Bible as it is written, to understand that immediately after the flood there was but one form of faith upon the earth, and that the true one. Noah was a preacher of righteousness both before and after the deluge, and because of their obedience to God's laws, he and his family were saved from the universal destruction that came upon the wicked. But their descendants, in an early day, began to depart from the purity of the truths that had saved "the fathers," and a knowledge of the forms of iniquity that existed amongst the antediluvians was in some manner conveyed to them, and incorporated in their debased new systems of worship. Noah, Melchizedek and others battled with but partial success against these growing infamies, and Abraham was especially called of the Lord to usher in a new dispensation. We have seen, in part, how he fulfilled this call; we shall now refer to some Gospel ideas that for many centuries afterwards were found incorporated amongst the filth and rubbish of paganism, some in Egypt, some in Persia, some in Chaldea, some in Greece, Rome and other nations. From this almost universal admixture of the true and the false it is evident that there was some primeval source from which the ancient gentile nations drew that which was good and true in their religions.

In our researches into the mythology of these peoples we find, amongst others, the following Gospel ideas:

The belief in the existence of one great father God.

The prophecy and expectation of the coming of a Son of God in the flesh.

A reverence for Adam as the great prince of his race, in some nations, extended to his worship as the father of the terrestrial gods.

The belief in a resurrection, and in future rewards and punishments.

The necessity of faith in the gods, and under certain very remarkable circumstances, to be hereafter noticed, of repentance and baptism.

The administration of washings and anointings.

Traditions, more or less perfect, of the great war in heaven when Lucifer and his angels were cast down upon the earth.

The belief in good and bad angels, ministers of the will of heaven.

A belief in the eternity of matter, and

The almost universal practice of sacrifice.

To give strength to the above assertions we shall now appeal to a number of well-known authors.

The Rev. Mr. Goodsir, in his work on Ethnic Inspiration, writes: "The principles of mythology enable us to discern the true order in which the various erroneous and morbid developments of human belief arose. It proves both that monotheism--the knowledge of the true God, preceded the various forms of polytheism, and especially the worship of the heavenly bodies; and that the worship of dead men preceded other forms of false or idolatrous worship; and the same facts which show that the worship of dead men was the first step in false religion, prove at the same time the original grafting of this on the belief of a heavenly Creator and Father. Were there no other than the single case of Egypt, as explained from its language, hieroglyphics and monuments, by Mr. Osborn, it would place the matter beyond all doubt, so clear and well-supported is that case. Adam and Eve, Noah and Tamer, Ham, Mizraim[14] and Phut were all deified there, while the supreme God was incontrovertibly known; and the sun was only a symbol and the supposed abode of Adam. There is reason to believe that the state of things in Chaldea and Babylon was substantially the same as this."

To this we may append the remark that the Egyptians appear to have recognized the partial truth that there be "that are called gods, whether in heaven or on earth, as there be gods many and lords many," but were ignorant of the corollary, "but to us there is but one God the Father." (1 Corinthians, viii, v. 5, 6.)

It must be evident from the light thown on the early history of the world, more especially of Egypt, by the Book of Abraham, that under the almost universally existing form of patriarchal government that "the fathers" were not only High Priests unto God by right of their "fatherhood," but also the kings of the earth by that same right,[15] and it was 0ne of the easiest things in the world for the descendants of these men, who ruled by right divine, to not only reverence them as ministers of heaven's will in all things, temporal and spiritual, but also to deify and afterwards worship them. Indeed in the case of most of these holy

[14] Mizriam is identified with Osiris, chief lord of the land of the departed.

[15] Max Muller says "king" originally meant "father."

patriarchs it was but a very small step in advance of their true position in relation to the sons of men; for "He called them Gods unto whom the word of God came, and the scriptures cannot be broken." (John, x, 35.)

We next appeal to Mr. Osborn, author of "The Religions of the World." In writing of the Egyptian mythology, he states: "This most ancient mythology, as described by authors who lived before the Christian era, and as set forth on the walls of the temples in which its ritual or worship was performed, was taught to the initiated and concealed from the vulgar, that God created all things at the first by the primary emanation from himself, his firstborn, who was the author and giver of all knowledge in heaven and on earth, being at the same time the wisdom and the word of God. The birth of this all-powerful being, his manifestation as an infant, his nurture and education through all the succeeding periods of childhood and of boyhood, constituted the grand mystery of the entire system." So convinced were the priests of this people of the coming of a Son of God, that they had chambers prepared in their temples for his nativity.

Another quotation from Mr. Osborn will, we trust, make the matter yet clearer to our readers. He says: "The founders of the nation knew not only of Ham and Mizriam, but of various men and women contemporary with, them, even of our first parents, Adam and Eve, as well as of our second progenitors, Noah and his wife Tamer. Adam has thus been handed down to us as Athom, the guide or governor of the sun; Eve as Hathor, who presided over the moon; Noah as Nuh, who presided over the Nile; while Ham, Mizraim, Phut, Neveth, or Neith, the wife of Ham, and others, occupied singular and sometimes multiform positions and offices in the Egyptian Pantheon."[16]

We will now leave modern writers, and draw attention to that wonderful papyrus, the Ancient Egyptian Ritual or Book of the Dead, and from its hieroglyphics show the relation in which Adam stood in their mythology, reminding our readers that the abode of the great father of humanity was supposed by them to be the sun, and that the chief seat of his worship was at Heliopolis, the city of the sun, the On of the Scriptures, Aseniath, a daughter of one of whose priests was married to Joseph, the son of Jacob.

---

[16] "Religions of the World."

Our extracts are necessarily brief, and simply intended to prove the trustworthiness of the quotations already made.

In the fifteenth chapter it is written :

"The praise of Athom[17] when he sets from the land of life, saith the Osir,[18]

"Glory be to Athom, setting from the gate of life,

"When his colors glow in the western gate of the horizon,

"Hail to thee setting from the land of life,

"Thou father of the Gods."

Again, (chapter xvii,) Adam is represented as saying:

"I am the great God, creating myself;

"I am the great Phoenix which is in On;

"I am the creator of beings and existences."

In another place it proclaims:

"Glory be to thee, O Sun; glory be to thee, O Athom,

"When thou goest down, perfect, crowned and glorious."

Adam is also called "the old man whose palace is at On," the "God alone in the firmament," "Father Athom," "Righteous Athom," and much more. Probably were we better versed in the mysteries of its hieroglyphics and idioms, the translation of this wonderful testimony to the belief of the ancients in the immortality of the soul, which this ritual is, would be yet plainer and more instructive. As it is, much of its imagery is very difficult for modern minds to grasp.

---

[17] The Egyptian form of the name Adam.
[18] The deceased.

From the Egyptians we will turn to the Persians, the people next most likely to show traces in their religion of the influence left by the preaching of the Gospel in patriarchal days. Mr. Hyde, in his "Religion of the Ancient Persians," points out how that Magianism, as set forth in its sacred books, taught that the human race sprang from a single pair; that it bore testimony to the occurrence of the flood; that it mentions Noah and his sons; that as far as Abraham is concerned, it declares him to have been its own author; and that it makes mention also of Moses. Moreover, it contains predictions respecting the appearance on earth of a Savior, who would ultimately overthrow the kingdom of darkness and make supreme and universal the kingdom of light and of God. It also taught the existence of good and of bad angels, also a resurrection of the dead.

The religions of ancient Greece and Rome were, to a very great extent, originally drawn from those of Egypt, Persia and Phoenicia. Many traces of Gospel principles can be found in them, hidden concealed under the mass of filth and abomination that in later ages disgraced the religions of the kingdoms of brass and iron. Still, in all these nations it is admitted that "so far from atheism and godless irreligion being the rule, belief in the Divine, however mistaken, and worship of the Divine, however superstitious, everywhere prevailed." With regard to special Gospel ideas prevailing in all these nations, it has been remarked that "baptism was as completely a portion of the primeval ceremonial worship as was the tenet of immortality and resurrection a portion of the primeval creed." It is also noticeable that all the Greek schools of philosophy taught the doctrine of the eternity of matter, and not only had these races a knowledge of things that occurred in antediluvian days, but in their different, absurd ways they recounted the history of the war in heaven when Lucifer was cast out. Those curious on this point can read their accounts of the war between the Titians and Heaven, and of the giants against Jupiter.

Late discoveries at Nineveh have demonstrated that the Chaldeans had also a very distinct tradition of this pre-Adamite war, as many particulars relating thereto have been found transcribed on the earthen tiles exhumed from the mounds where that once mighty city is supposed to have stood. These tablets having been translated by Mr. Geo. Smith, of the British Museum, prove to be an account of the war in heaven before the creation of this earth, of the fall of man, of the flood, the building of the tower of Babel, etc. The similarity between the statements on these cuneiform records and the Bible account of the same events is very remarkable and interesting, while at the same time they prove how wide spread in ancient times was the knowledge of God's dealings with humanity.

CHAPTER 5

THE ANCIENT PAGAN MYSTERIES.--THEIR HISTORY AND INTENT.--THE CIRCULAR PLATE IN THE BOOK OF ABRAHAM.--ITS PUPORT AND USE.

WE now turn to another interesting feature of this phase of the subject.

In the explanation given by the Prophet Joseph of the disc or circular cut accompanying the Book of Abraham, he states: "Fig. 3 is made to represent God sitting upon his throne, clothed with power and authority, with a crown of eternal light upon his head, representing, also, the grand key words of the holy priesthood, as revealed to Adam in the Garden of Eden, as also to Seth, Noah, Melchisedek, Abraham, and all to whom the priesthood was revealed." Fig. 7 also contains "the grand key words of the Priesthood." God having delivered these powers of the heavenly kingdom to "all to whom the priesthood was revealed," until Abraham's day, it would be but natural to suppose that as men gradually departed from the truth they would still endeavor to retain these sacred trusts in their midst; and however much they might depart from the purity of the faith proclaimed and practised by the ancient patriarchs they would still strive to perpetuate the knowledge these "keys" conveyed, that they might have a claim on the blessings of the world to come. It is so natural to humanity to claim the blessings of God's word long after they have ceased to regard its obligations.

The fact of these things appearing in the Book of Abraham, written in hieroglyphics, renders it very supposable that at one time the import of these revelations was comprehended by those among the Egyptians who received the teachings of Abraham; and so far as Jewish tradition is concerned, it is full of references to these matters, though these latter, perhaps, more directly centre in the rites of the temples at Jerusalem. It is our province to show that the recollection of these things was sought to be perpetuated amongst the heathen--originating, as usual, in Egypt long after the greater portion of that which was pure and holy in the principles with which these things had been associated, by the ministers of the word of Jehovah, was lost sight of in the teachings and practices of these gentile nations. To do this we must call attention to the so-called secret "mysteries" of the ancients, which, to us, seem clearly, in their origin, to have been attempts to imitate the administrations of the holy priesthood, in the sacred rites appertoining to the fulness of the Gospel. In the investigation of this point we are greatly indebted to M. Faber's researches into the "Mysteries of the Cabiri," and to other authors who have enlarged upon his researches.

According to one of the gentlemen above referred to, "some of these mysteries were expressly instituted, as there is good reason to believe, to preserve in remembrance the remains of pure primeval faith and worship." Another states, "every ancient people possessed its mysteries, which had for their object to uphold the religious truths that animate the hope of immortality, or in which were observed rites intended to explain and enforce the conduct suitable to those who cherished and wished to realize that hope." What took place in the administration of these mysteries is very difficult for the inquirer to discover, for they were "conducted in secret, and those who were permitted to take part in them were solemnly obliged not to divulge what they had seen and learned," the word mystery itself being derived from a Greek word signifying to "shut the lips." However, from what can be learned it is believed that the initiated were "powerfully appealed to by scenic or other modes of representing the condition of the good and bad." According to a writer in the American Cyclopaedia, "they consisted, in general, of rites of purification and expiation, of sacrifices and processions, of ecstatic or orgiastic songs and dances, of nocturnal festivals fit to impress the imagination, and of spectacles designed to excite the most diverse emotions, terror and trust, and sorrow and joy, hope and despair. The celebration was chiefly by symbolical acts and spectacles, yet sacred mystical words, formulas, fragments of liturgies or hymns were also employed. There were likewise certain objects with which occult meanings, that were imparted to the initiated, were associated, or which were used in the various ceremonies in the ascending scale of initiation. The sacred phrases, concerning which silence was imposed, were themselves symbolical legends, and probably not statements of speculative truths." St. Croix, on this subjects, writes: "The germ of the mysteries is lustration," (or purification by water) "and expiation. The doctrines taught were the necessity of repentance and confession, the immortality of the soul, and a future state of rewards and punishments." The Sr. De Sacy adds, "certain rites and symbols were secret, and these it was sacrilege to reveal." Baur states, "the fundamental idea of the mysteries is that of a god who suffers and dies and afterwards triumphs over death, and has a glorious resurrection." Regarding the Persian mysteries of Mythras, it has been written: "The initiation was protracted and severe. The neophyte was baptized, anointed on the forehead and received bread and wine; a crown was placed on his head."

With regard to the preparation needed from those who asked admission to these rites the very remarkable statement is made: "It is quite undoubted respecting them, that as a necessary condition to admission, and as an important part of initiation, two things were imperatively necessary, namely a confession of sins, a promise of amendment of life, followed by baptism in some form more or less complete." Faber states "baptism continued to be handed down in all the mysteries," whilst another writer affirms that "continence, fasting and lustrations" were necessary pre-requisites before the applicant could enter the sacred doors. It is also a fact worthy of consideration that in a list of forty-five sacred Greek words gathered by M. Faber, there is scarcely one which does not resemble the Hebrew term for the same or a similar object.

As the ages roll round these mysteries degenerated into the most licentious orgies, where excesses of a disgraceful character were so shamelessly practiced that in some cases they fell under the ban of the law, though presumedly a portion of the worship of the gods. As an example of this we will take the mysteries of Dionysus. These were originally celebrated by women alone, in the temple of Dionysus. They were presided over by the wife of the Archon king (Basilissa), assisted by fourteen priestesses, to whom she took an oath that she was pure and unpolluted, and with whom she offered mystic sacrifices for the welfare of the city. When these mysteries were introduced into Rome, they speedily degenerated into shameful immoralities; men, as well as women were initiated; and such were the crimes and excesses committed that they were at length suppressed by a senatus consult, B. 0. 186 (Livy, xxxix, 8 to 18).

It has been urged as an argument against the veracity of the translation by the Prophet Joseph Smith, of the circular cut or disc, but why, we cannot comprehend, that numerous copies of it exist, scattered among the museums of Europe. These copies have been found buried with mummies in the same way as the one that fell into the Prophet's hands. Instead of being an argument against the truthfulness of the translation given by Joseph Smith, we consider it a very strong one in its favor. For this reason, Egyptiologists acknowledge that some peculiar potency was ascribed to it by the ancient Egyptians, but their ideas are very vague as to in what that power consisted. It was customary with the ancient inhabitants of Egypt, to enshroud their dead in hieroglyphic wrappings, on which various facts relating to the life of the deceased were narrated. This writing was addressed to Osiris, the chief lord of Amend, the land of the departed, and amongst other things it stated that the acts of the Osir, the deceased, had been scrutinized by the seven inquisitors appointed to investigate the lives of men, and that he was found worthy to pass by those who guarded the gates of the eternal worlds, and partake of the blessings of the saved. Accompanying the mummy is also often found this sacred disc, or hypociphilas, as the learned term it, which, if we mistake not, was usually placed under or near the head of the mummy. The translations given by the professedly learned convey no idea why this was so placed, but the revelation through our martyred Prophet, that it contains the key words of the holy priesthood, at once makes the reason plain. The Egyptians buried this disc containing these sacred words with their dead, for very much the same reason that the Saints bury their dead in the robes of the holy priesthood. No doubt the true meaning of these key words was soon lost from amongst the Egyptians, but they knew enough to understand something of their value, and as ages rolled on, their apostate priesthood doubtlessly invented some myth to take their place. That these priests did claim to hold such keys, is clearly shown in a photograph in the Deseret Museum, of the walls of the Temple at Karnac, on which the gods are represented, each holding a key in his hand.

CHAPTER 6

THE CHRONLOGY OF THE ANCIENTS.--A KEY TO ITS MYSTERIES.--THE ANTEDILUVIAN MONARCHS.--JOSEPHUS AND CHINESE CHRONOLOGY.--ABRAHAM ON PHARAOH'S THRONE.--HE MAKES A TREATY ENDING A ONE HUNDREAD YEARS WAR.--CHEOPS.

IN the seventh paragraph of the Book of Abraham we find the following: "Now the first government of Egypt was established by Pharaoh, the eldest son of Egyptus, the daughter of Ham, and it was after the manner of the government of Ham, which was patriarchal, Pharaoh being a righteous man, established his kingdom and judged his people wisely and justly all his days, seeking earnestly to imitate that order established by the fathers in the first generations, in the days of the first patriarchal reign, even in the reign of Adam, and also of Noah, his father, who blessed him with the blessings of the earth, and with the blessings of wisdom, but cursed him as pertaining to the priesthood." The next paragraph is as follows: "Now Pharaoh being of that lineage by which he could not have the priesthood, notwithstanding the Pharaohs would fain claim it from Noah, through Ham, therefore my father was led away by their idolatry; but I shall endeavor, hereafter, to delineate the chronology, running back from myself to the beginning of the creation, for the records have come into my hands, which I hold unto this present time."

We desire to draw attention to several ideas advanced in the above quotations.

1st. That the early Egyptians were acquainted with events that occurred before the flood.

2d. That the antediluvian patriarchs reigned in the midst of their descendants as kings.

3d. That this form of government was the prevailing one, in the days immediately succeeding the deluge.

4th. That the Egyptians established in their midst an imitation or bogus priesthood, that rapidly carried the people into idolatry.

5th. That Abraham, and probably many others, possessed records running back to the beginning of time.

Modern research has amply vindicated the statements of Abraham's record with regard to the condition of society amongst the early dwellers on the banks of the Nile. Listen to what Mr. Osborn states on this subject, and, though in different wording, note how fully he bears out the patriarch's assertions. Mr. O. remarks in his "Religions of the "World," that "Egyptian remains prove clearly that, while to all appearance the first settlers in Egypt carried along with them some germinal forms of very malignant religious error, they carried with them, in addition to the mere ancestral or genealogical and historical knowledge, a most deep experimental knowledge and conviction of the reality of divine being and agency, and a knowledge also of that form in which, from the time of the Fall, the revelation of the most important elements of religion appears to have been imparted to mankind."

We shall not attempt to establish the ideas from the Book of Abraham, above noticed, in the order in which they are placed, but before leaving this branch of the subject, we believe that we shall be able to adduce sufficient evidence to convince all who are willing to learn the truth, that Abraham's statements as given by the Prophet Joseph are historically correct.

The fact of Abraham coming in possession of certain genealogical records may seem somewhat incredible to those who have not studied the subject. Many are too apt to consider the people of those early ages as but one step removed from barbarians, being, if we sense their idea correctly, very much on a par with the modern Tartar or Bedouin Arab; and the thought of such a people possessing a literature seems to be inconceivable to the minds of many otherwise intelligent people. But have such ever noticed that the Bible, in one of its very first chapters, actually speaks of "the book of generations of Adam," (Genesis v. 1,) and it is from that book apparently that Moses' genealogical record of the antediluvians was transcribed. In confirmation of the existence of such a book, Josephus states that those who lived before the flood "noted down, with great accuracy, both the births and deaths of illustrious men," (Josephus, book 1, chap. 3,) which record would undoubtedly be preserved among the royal archives, and as such, being deemed of the utmost value as giving the genealogy of the kings, be saved by Noah in the ark, he, according to Abraham and Josephus, also being the reigning sovereign at the time of the deluge. Josephus specifically states that "that calamity happened in the six hundredth year of Noah's government." (Josephus, book 1, chap. 3.) In fact Josephus gives a list of the antediluvian monarchs, or patriarchs, as they are termed in the Bible, but the fact that he recognized them as the sovereigns of the antediluvian world is very strong corroborative testimony of the statement of Abraham that Adam and Noah reigned as kings over their fellow men. The following is Josephus' statement with regard to this matter: (Josephus, book 1, chap. 3.)

"Seth was born when Adam was in his 230th year, who lived 930 years. Seth begat Enoch in his 205th year, who, when he lived 912 years, delivered the government to Canaan, his son, whom he had at his 119th year. He lived 905 years. Canaan, when he had lived 910 years, had his son Mahalaleel, who was born in his 170th year. This Mahalaleel, having lived 895 years, died, leaving his son Jared, whom he begat when he was at his 165th year. He lived 962 years and then his son Enoch succeeded him, who was born when his father was 162 years old. Now he, when he had lived 365 years, departed and went to God, whence it is that they have not written down his death. Now Methuselah, the son of Enoch, who was born to him when he was 165 years old, had Lamech for his son, when he was 187 years of age, to whom he delivered the government when he had retained it 969 years. Now Lamech, when he had governed 777 years, appointed Noah, his son, to be the ruler of the people, who was born to Lamech when he was 182 years old, and retained the government 950 years."

We here draw attention to a somewhat remarkable coincidence. It is that the length of the reigns of these patriarchs, as given by Josephus, agrees, with one exception, we believe, with the length of their lives according to Bible chronology, but what makes this feature more remarkable is that Josephus does exactly the same thing as the Chinese do in their antediluvian chronology. "The Chinese account speaks of ten dynasties of superior beings, who ruled in their country 1,000 years each before the sky fell on the earth (i.e. the flood). It is not hard to see that this is only a different and a singular manner of relating the same facts. * * * Moses informs us that each of these ten generations did extend near a thousand years, but he let us know that a son and his father walked much of their earthly race together. The journey of each was long, but it was a simultaneous travel."[19]

Now, we think that the statement of Abraham turns a key by which a flood of light is thrown on the early history of the first nations that came into being after the flood, for instance, the Egyptian, the Chaldean, and the Chinese. Scientists and religionists have been wrangling for scores of years with regard to the chronology of these nations, both parties, as a rule, seeming to take it for granted that these chronological records should stop at the flood, presumedly for the reason that all mankind but one family of eight were then destroyed. As there is incontrovertible evidence that the ancients were acquainted with facts and events relating to the earth and the heavens long anterior to the generally accepted date of the deluge, skeptics have loudly expressed their doubts as to the flood having occurred at all. But when we take into consideration the fact that those who were saved were the royal family--the king and queen, with their three sons and the princesses, their wives--and that this king (Noah) ruled after as well as before the flood, it remains no longer a wonder how these nations traced their existence to years long anterior to that dire calamity. To them it was a terrible disaster in the history of their nation, nothing more; there was no break in the royal descent, the same king reigned before and after it took place, the same dynasty remained in power, his son succeeded to the throne; the royal records were preserved, and the Egyptians, the Chaldeans, and the Chinese alike with natural national pride all claimed the sovereigns who ruled from Adam to Noah as the kings of their peculiar nation. Their records were like three converging lines, centering at Noah, and from him continuing backward in one and the same straight line to Adam. To illustrate: let us suppose a case. We will imagine that a vast desolation sweeps over the empire of Germany. The king and the three princes, with their families, alone are saved from its fatal horrors. By and by, these three princes establish thrones of their own, say, one in Prussia, one in Pomerania, and one in Hanover. Would the national historians of future ages, when these three kingdoms had become great and populous, stop in their respective national histories at the date that this overwhelming catastrophe occurred? Would it not be much more reasonable to conclude that they would accumulate the histories of this and former epochs and continue their accounts through this calamity to the earliest days their records would reach. We think so, and in this way we discover an easy and reasonable solution to the

[19] Nelson's "Infidelity, its Cause and Cure."

difficulties that beset Chinese and Egyptian chronology, and are able to account for the interminable lists of kings that grace their annals. In fact, so far as Egypt is concerned, it had no consecutive chronology. This truth is now admitted by the most learned in that branch of science. But they undoubtedly carried their records, in a jumbled up way, back beyond the flood, (probably obtaining some information thereon from the records in the possession of Abraham,) and in postdiluvian days they, in vanity, inserted the names of scores of princes who reigned contemporaneously in various parts of the Valley of the Nile. Admit these two facts, and the solution is found to the mysteries of Egyptian chronology, what they had of it. Again, why should we permit the descendants of Shem, as in the case of the Hebrews, to monopolize their antediluvian progenitors. These men were the fathers of all mankind, and all had equal right to claim them as their own.

Considerable ridicule has been needlessly expended on the statement that the sitting figure in Plate III, of the Book of Abraham, represents that patriarch "sitting upon Pharaoh's throne by the politeness of the king." It has been scoffed at as an idea entirely too silly to be met with calm argument. To imagine that the great and mighty ruler of Egypt would invite an "Arab Sheik," at best a shepherd prince, to sit upon his throne, was altogether too absurd for a moment's serious consideration; such extraordinary condescension would shame a Chesterfield. But we all know that it is often as easy to ridicule as it is difficult to disprove; so we will let the scoffer jest, whilst we bring forward our "strong reasons" for believing this, as well as all other portions of Abraham's divinely inspired record. Josephus writes (Antiquities, book 1, chap, viii,) that when Pharaoh discovered that the woman, Sarah, whom he desired to take into his household, was the wife of Abraham, he made, as an excuse for his action, that believing her to be the patriarch's sister he wished to marry her, from his desire to be related to so distinguished a personage as Abraham. This could not be irony; Pharaoh was not in a condition to be ironical with his guest. It must have been an excuse that bore upon its face the probability of truth, and one that would be accepted as genuine by the powerful visitor from Canaan. Had it been otherwise, it would have been adding insult to injury, and instead of Abraham remaining in Egypt to become a teacher to its people, we should probably learn that in anger he returned to his own land. Then, accepting Pharaoh's own statement to be true, is it difficult to believe that he who wished to be so nearly allied to Abraham, would, in the fulness of Eastern politeness, think it any too great a condescension to ask him to sit upon his throne, whilst he explained to him and to his court the wonders of the numberless creations of God?

Nor is this all; we have yet other testimony of how powerful a man was Abraham amongst the children of the Nile. Our readers will probably recollect that we have already drawn attention to a statement of Josephus, that at the time the patriarch visited Egypt, the people of that country despised each other's sacred rites, and were very angry one with another on that account; further, that Abraham proved to them that their various reasonings were vain and void of truth. Modern research has shown that Abraham did more than this. It appears that somewhat more than one hundred years before Abraham's advent into Egypt, one of its monarchs--Mencheres--attempted to establish the worship of Osiris over all Egypt. As a result, a great religious war ensued, which continued for a century. The history of the country at this time becomes involved and obscure in the highest degree, but one fact is absolutely certain, and that is, that this civil war was fierce, long continued and with varying success. A late British historical text book states that in the year 1984 B. C. (according to the best chronology, which is, however, far from satisfactory)[20] Abraham visited and aided Achthoes [Pharaoh] in forming a treaty with his rival to terminate the religious war. Then, if it be true that Abraham was so great a power in his day that by his aid a civil war of one hundred years' duration was brought to an amicable close, is there anything incongruous in the idea that he, by politeness, sat upon the throne of the ruler to whom he had been of so great service?

About this time, as near as can be told, a great change was effected in the religion of the Egyptians, which we ascribe to the preaching, in their midst, of the Gospel, by the Father of the Faithful. It appears from Herodotus, that according to the story of the idolatrous Egyptian priests of his day, that when Cheops ascended the throne he "closed the temples of the false gods, and prohibited their sacrifices"[21] Cheops is said to have reigned fifty years, and was succeeded by his brother Chepren, who also kept the temples closed. In the succeeding reign the temples were again opened, and the people returned to their old modes of worship. So hated were these two sovereigns by the heathen dwellers by the Nile, of later years, that Herodotus states that they would not even mention their names, Mr. John Taylor, author of "The Great Pyramid; why was it built

[20] Facts and Dates by Rev. A. Mackay, Edinburgh, 1870.
[21] Hartcourt's Doctrines of the Deluge.

and who built it?" from various evidences brought to his notice, infers that these kings "might have been pre-eminently good, or were at all events of different religious faith" from those who told the story to Herodotus. Putting the various facts before stated together, that Abraham taught holy principles to the Egyptians, that his teachings so wrought upon them that they brought to a close a civil war of one hundred years' duration, and that near this time the idolatrous temples were closed, all forming parts of one harmonious whole, we are irresistibly drawn to the conclusion that these changes were brought about by the proclamation of the Gospel; more especially are we led thereto by the hatred shown to the kings who accepted this message and carried out these reforms, by the worshipers of Osiris in succeeding generations. It so much resembles the course pursued by others in like circumstances in other lands and at other times. Cheops is usually credited with being the builder of the great pyramid, and to that mighty structure we shall by and by appeal for testimony to prove that whoever its builders were, they were acqainted with the sublime system of astronomy revealed by Jehovah to Abraham, with instructions to teach it to the Egyptians.

CHAPTER 7

THE MEANS BY WHICH ABRAHAM WAS TAUGHT ASTRONOMY.--THE ABRAHAMIC SYSTEM OF ASTRONOMY.--FROM THE EARTH TO KOLOB.--THE SYSTEM PROVEN TRUE BY RECENT RESEARCH.--TESTIMONY OR VARIOUS AUTHORS.--ALCYONE.--MR. PETRIE'S TESTIMONY.--ADMISSIONS THAT THE ANCIENTS WERE TAUGHT SCIENTIFIC TRUTHS BY DIVINE REVELATION.

A BRAHAM tells us that there were three ways by which he received his knowledge of astronomy.

1st. Through the records handed down to him from the antediluvian patriarchs.

2d. By the use of the Urim and Thummim, which he received from the Lord in Ur of Chaldea.

3d. By direct communication with the Almighty, who, face to face, and with His own voice, explained to him the laws that govern His countless creations.

The system of astronomy revealed by God to Abraham is so vast, so grand, so comprehensive, that no uninspired man ever searched out its depths or ascended its heights. Occasionally a patient searcher after truth caught a faint glimmer of its glory, but that was all. But they none learned as Abraham learned, nor did the profoundest astronomers of forty years ago have aught but the most meagre and vain conception of the truths given to the world by Joseph Smith in his inspired translation of Abraham's record. Indeed, the truths there set forth are, today, scarcely recognized by the more conservative schools of astronomy, it is only the more daring minds that accept them, even in part.

The great truths told by Abraham regarding the starry hosts of heaven are recorded thus: "I saw the stars that they were very great, and that one of them was nearest unto the throne of God; and there were many great ones that were near it; and the Lord said unto me, These are the governing ones: and the name of the great one is Kolob, because it is near unto me, for I am the Lord thy God; I have set this one to govern all those which belong to the same order of that upon which thou standest. And the Lord said unto me, by the Urim and Thummim, that Kolob was after the manner of the Lord, according to its times and seasons in the revolution thereof, that one revolution was a day unto the Lord, after his manner of reckoning, it being one thousand years according to the time appointed unto that whereon thou standest. This is the reckoning of the Lord's time, according to the reckoning of Kolob."

In other words these great, governing planets control all others in their revolutions, or are the centres around which the others revolve. As the moon revolves around the earth, and the earth with the other primary and secondary planets belonging to this solar system revolve around the sun, so has the sun a centre around which it, with all its earths and moons, revolves, while this grand centre has a governing planet also, a sun or world around which it, with its attendant systems of suns and worlds, revolves, and so on until we come to Kolob, the "nearest to the celestial or the residence of God," which is the grand centre which governs all the suns and systems of suns "which belong to the same order" as our earth and those that move with it.

Still further than this the Book of Abraham teaches us:

1st. That Kolob is the greatest of all the stars seen by that patriarch.

That it is so because it is nearest to the celestial, or residence of God.

That it is nigh unto the throne of God.

That it governs all the planets which belong to the same order as this earth.

That it is after the reckoning of the Lord's time.

That it is after the manner of the Lord according to its times and seasons and the revolutions thereof.

That one revolution is a day unto the Lord.

That one day, in Kolob, is equal to a thousand years, according to the measurement of this earth.

That Kolob signifies first creation.

That it is the first in government, and last pertaining to the measurement of time. The measurement according to celestial time; which celestial time signifies one day to a cubit.

2d. That Oliblish stands next to Kolob.

That it is the next grand governing creation.

That it is equal to Kolob in its revolution and in its measurement of time.

That it holds the key of power as pertaining to other planets.

3d. That Enish-go-on-dosh is also a governing planet, which was said, by the ancient Egyptians, to be the sun, and to borrow (receive) its light from Kolob through the medium of Kae-e-vanrash.

4th. That Kae-e-vanrash is the grand key, or governing power, which governs fifteen other fixed planets or stars, as also the moon (Floeese), the earth and the sun in their annual revolutions. That Kae-e-vanrash receives its power through Kli-flos-is-es or Hah-ko-kau-beam.

5th. Kli-flos-is-es and

6th. Hah-ko-kau-beam receive their light from the revolutions of Kolob.

To summarize: That this solar system is governed by Kae-e-vanrash, which is governed by Kli-flos-is-es or Hah-ko-kau-beam, which are governed by Kolob. Whether Oliblish belongs to the same order of systems as this earth, or simply holds the keys of power-pertaining to other planets, is not so apparent.

When Joseph Smith enunciated the sublime truths above noticed no such thoughts were prevalent amongst the students of astronomy. The

Herschels had some inkling of the facts, but their ideas were crude and undeveloped. It was not until the Book of Abraham had been published in America, and if we mistake not in England also, that Sir Wm. G. Hamilton, of the Dublin University, advanced the idea that our solar system had a centre around which the sun and all its attendant planets moved. To-day the scholars in the most radical school of astronomy will only admit that our system has a centre, and that the probabilities are that that centre has a centre also round which it and all its satellites move. Further than this they cannot go. However, the little they do admit, confirms the mighty truths revealed to Abraham of old and Joseph of today. On the other hand, the followers of the more conservative schools will simply acknowledge that our solar system has a proper motion of its own, independent of its relative or apparent motions with regard to other stars. They admit that "relative to the general mass of stars, our sun is moving in the direction of the constellation of Hercules." They have come to this conclusion, because they find that the stars in that part of the heavens are continually growing brighter, (thus showing they are coming nearer,) whilst those in exactly the

opposite direction are as continually growing more dim. They have also discovered that "there are in the heavens several cases of widely extended groups of stars, having a common proper motion entirely different from that of She stars around and among them. Such groups they say "must form connected systems,"[22] or in other words, are all controlled by one and the same governing planet. It is also admitted that "the stars in all parts of the heavens move in all directions with all sorts of velocities;[23] but they claim that the distances of the stars from the earth are so immense, and so short a period of time has elapsed since they first began to notice these movements, that they cannot with certainty say whether they are moving in circles or straight lines, it is only by analogy that they reason that they are moving around a centre. So little are some of these observers willing to admit, that Prof. Newcomb simply allows that "as our sun is merely one of the stars, and rather a small one too, it may have a proper motion as well as other stars." The Smithsonian report for 1871, speaking of Herschel, says: "The world can afford to wait. Astronomy advances. It may be, in the distant future, that the mysterious centre around which our sun and his worlds revolve, may be detected and

---

[22] "Popular Astronomy, 1878," by 'Professor 8. Newcomb, of the United States Naval Observatory.

[23] Ibid.

afford a solution for other mysteries as well as these. The greatest astronomer is equipped for no more than a Sabbath-day's journey." Another writer remarks, "Madler attempted to show, from an examination of the proper motions of the stars, that the whole stellar universe was revolving around Alcyone, of the Pleiades (or 'seven stars') as a centre--a theory, the grandeur of which led to its wide diffusion in popular writing." Mr. Wm. Petrie, of London, writing with regard to this same star says: "Alcyone, a primeval name of the star, means the centre, and has quite recently been discovered to be really the centre around which even our whole solar system, amongst others, revolves."

Short as is this last quotation, it testifies to three things confirmatory of the divine inspiration that gave to the world the Book of Abraham.

1st. That this solar system has a central or governing sun or planet.

2d. That this fact was known to the ancients, who gave to this particular star the name of the centre.

3d. That in modern times this truth has only been "quite recently discovered." That is to say; Joseph Smith could not have learned it from living men or modern books, but only through the revelations of God.

And here let us observe that the word planet, as given by Joseph Smith to the suns, in common parlance called fixed stars, is scientifically correct, as a planet is a world that moves or wanders through space, and the common nomenclature of fixed stars is untruthful and scientifically incorrect, as none are absolutely at a standstill or fixed immovably in one place.

Elder Joseph L. Barfoot affords us the following additional particulars with regard to the revolution of the solar system around Alcyone. He states: "The entire march of our sun and its system around its centre is 25,868 years. (The period of the precession of the equinoxes.) I believe this to be the period of the solar orbit, and that there is some relation to this period and the sacred cubit (25.025) which may yet be discovered. The change of 50.1" per annum in the appearance of the stars as seen from the earth results from the orbital motion around Kolob or some other large body. This would be a degree in seventy-two years. Of course the orbit would be immense; the Lord evidently gave the Prophet

Joseph an insight into the order of this grand eternal round, which I think is really pictured in the Hypocephalus.

"The earth rotates on its axis, and moves in its orbit by the power imparted to its mass by the solar forces; the deflective force from the line of the sun's motion, produced by the sun's rotation on its axis, and its progression around the centre of momentum of the system to which it belongs. And, since neither the earth, nor any other body of matter, has power without motion, so, in the sun's great power, we have evidence of its great progressive motion. The rotation of the sun of more than 6,500 feet per second would demand a velocity of progression of over 26,000 feet per second. Herschel, by observation, was led to conclude that 'the sun somehow moved towards Hercules with the velocity of the earth, or 100,000 feet per second,' and to infer that the sun actually describes 'a great orbit around some undiscriminated centre.' Sir R. Phillips analogically estimated the size of this orbit, and announced that with equal centripetal and centrifugal force, it would require an orbit of 162,885 millions of miles, performed in exactly 25,868 years, the period of the precession of the equinoxes.

"And as the earth and the other planets of this system rotate by reason of the central solar motion, and turn on their axis by being deflected from a right line in their respective orbits, Philips has shown that the sun and all other planets rotate, as a result of the operation of the same law of motion, and the fact that its satellites move in elliptical (egg-shaped, to be exact) orbits shows that the solar centre is advancing.

"That this earth is part of a system that suffers no permanent change, is seen in the unvarying order of the eclipses, which return in periods of eighteen years and eleven days, if there are four leap years, and in eighteen years and ten days, if there are five leap years in the period. And although astronomy does not yet recognize the different orders of planets alluded to in the Book of Abraham, the teachings of science are all tending to show that there are great governing, central forces and periodic cycles."

Having thus shown that present research and investigation are proving the astronomical truths first given to this generation by that unlearned but heaven-inspired man, the Prophet Joseph Smith, we have next to show that the Egyptians were familiar with them, and that they learned them through the teachings of Abraham. To have done this some fifteen or twenty years ago would have been next to an impossibility; but to-day, through the researches of various talented and earnest men, it can be demonstrated with comparative ease.

But before we attempt to prove that Abraham was actually the instrument used of God to instruct the Egyptians in the mysteries of the starry worlds, we will present a few extracts, from various writers, to manifest that even the scientific world is beginning to admit that the Egyptians obtained their knowledge of astronomy through divine agency or revelation, as it was entirely out of their power in those early postdiluvian days to make such stupendous advances in this science with the instruments and learning then at their disposal, without they received such aid from records, etc., of antediluvian times.

Rev. Mr. Mackay, referring to some of the astronomical truths known to the ancient inhabitants of the land of the Pharaohs, states that he believes they were "revealed to man, ages and generations before science had any existence," and strange to say, the truths to which this gentleman refers have a direct relation to those contained in the Book of Abraham. Mr. Wm. Osborn, in a sketch of the history of ancient Egypt, remarks: "According to Moses, moreover, the age that produced by far the most remarkable of those monuments (the pyramids) was one in which the Almighty had frequent and familiar intercourse with man, as in the case of the patriarchs, Abraham, Melchizedek and Job; while the monument itself evinces innumerable evidences of a knowledge and wisdom to which unaided humanity has nowhere ever attained."

Rev. Mr. Goodsir, from the demonstration of facts akin to the foregoing, remarks: "The conclusion that some men in primeval times were taught by God, for important religious and moral purposes, scientific truths which modern men of science are only now discovering, is maintained on the strength of two lines of evidence--first, the freedom of scripture rightly interpreted from scientific error, and from the religious and moral errors witnessed among the pagans as the result of ignorance and errors in science: and second, the possession by primeval man of such scientific knowledge as we are only now reaching, as demonstrated by the great pyramid. Certain things render it extremely probable that this knowledge was imparted to the Ethnics [the gentiles] (who employed it in constructing the great pyramid) by servants of God, whom He had taught; and though ultimately corrupted and obscured by the pagans, still it is highly probable that, evincing its truth even from the midst of enveloping error, this scientific knowledge continued to stimulate the Egyptian, and afterwards the Greek, mind to scientific inquiry. * * * For as there is the clearest evidence that a revelation of religious truth existed in primeval times, and continued to benefit men, even when it became more or less corrupted, so is there as clear evidence that men were primevally instructed in the most important cosmologic and scientific truths. * * * The extreme probability is that a true scientific conception of the Kosmos in general would be at first conveyed to man directly by God, to guard his intelligent and highly-favored child from nature worship."

That God did use Abraham, as stated in his book, to convey astronomical knowledge to the Egyptians, is, we think, fully demonstrated by the following: Josephus (book 1, chapter viii,) states that Abraham "communicated to them (the Egyptians) arithmetic, and delivered to them the science of astronomy, for before Abraham came into Egypt they were unacquainted with those parts of learning, for that science came by the Chaldeans into Egypt, and from them to the Greeks also."

This is very strong corroborative testimony, but modern research actually claims to have discovered the year in which Abraham did this. The British text book already referred to, entitled "Facts and Dates," published in 1870 by the well-known firm of Wm. Blackwood & Sons, of Edinburgh (we are particular in giving details, to show that it proceeds from a reliable and highly respectable firm), in its history of ancient Egypt, gives the following:

"B.C. 1980. Abraham teaches the king of Egypt the true chronology, after which the inscriptions bear the name of the year and month."

So far as the actual year is concerned, we deem it a matter of minor importance, so that the fact is acknowledged, and the truth of modern revelation vindicated.

CHAPTER 8

ABRAHAM AS A PYRAMID BUILDER.--PHILITION.--THE USES OF THE PYRAMIDS.--THE COFFER A BAPTISMAL FONT.-- SYMBOLISM IN BAPTISM FRO THE DEAD.--THE SACRED CUBIT.--"ONE DAY TO A CUBIT."--ALCYONE.--THE SUN'S DISTANCE.--PYRAMID REFERENCES TO ASTRONOMICAL TRUTHS.--SUMMARY OF PYRAMID REFERENCES.

T'HE next task which we have assigned ourselves, is to show from the ancient pyramid of Cheops that the true system of astronomy, as taught by God to Abraham, was known to those who raised this mighty structure. To do this we desire to draw attention and consider separately three points.

1st. The historical reasons we have for believing that Abraham superintended the erection of this pyramid.

2d. The reasons why this vast structure was built, and the uses for which it was designed.

3d. The direct evidences from the dimensions, form, etc., of the pyramid of Cheops, that tend to prove that its builders were acquainted with the laws that govern the starry worlds.

The Pharaoh, or king of Egypt, who is generally regarded as the builder of the first pyramid, is known to secular history by the name of Cheops. To him and his actions in closing the idolatrous temples of Egypt, we have referred in a previous chapter, as well as to the statement of Herodotus, that the Egyptians so detested his memory that they would not even mention his name. Hence he states, "they commonly call the pyramids after Philition,[24] a shepherd, who at that time fed his flocks about the place." Remarking upon the above statement, Mr. Proctor, the celebrated astronomer, writes: "The mention of the shepherd Philition, who fed his flocks about the place where the great Pyramid was built, is a singular feature of Herodotus' narrative. It reads like some strange misinterpretation of the story related to him by the Egyptian priests. It is

[24] It is worthy of note that the root of the name Philition or Philitis signifies a lover of truth, a most appropriate name for Abraham.

obvious if the word Philition did not represent a people, but a person, this person must have been very eminent and distinguished--a shepherd king--not a mere shepherd. Rawlinson suggests that Philitis was probably a shepherd prince from Palestine, perhaps of Philistine descent. Prof. Smyth comes to the conclusion that some She-mite prince, 'a contemporary of, but rather older than the patriarch Abraham,' visited Egypt at this time and obtained such influence over the mind of Cheops as to persuade him to erect the pyramid. According to Smyth, the prince was no other than Melchizedek, king of Salem, and the influence he exerted was supernatural. * * * It seems tolerably clear that certain shepherd chiefs who came into Egypt during Cheops' reign were connected in some way with the designing of the great pyramid. It is clear also that they were men of a different religion from the Egyptians, and persauded Cheops to abandon the religion of his people."

If Josephus be correct, Professor Smyth's deductions regarding Melchizedek are wrong, for the former says that the Egyptians were taught astronomy by Abraham; without Melchizedek followed Abraham into Egypt instead of preceding him, which, though possible, we have no account of in any of the sacred writings.

Mr. Proctor further writes: "In the first place, the history of the pyramids shows that the erection of the first great pyramid was in all probability either suggested to Cheops by wise men who visited Egypt from the east, or else some important information conveyed to him by such visitors caused him to conceive the idea of building the pyramid. In either case we may suppose, as the history indeed suggests, that these learned men, whoever they may have been, remained in Egypt to superintend the erection of the structure. * * * The astronomical peculiarities which form so significant a portion of the great pyramid were probably provided for entirely under the direction of the shepherd chiefs who had exerted so strange an influence upon the mind of king Cheops. * * * It is certain in any case that they [the shepherd chiefs] were opposed to idolatry; and we have thus some means of inferring who they were or whence they came. We know that one particular branch of one particular race in the east was characterized by a most marked hatred of idolatry in all its forms. * * * And the Bible record shows that members of this Chaldean family visited Egypt from time to time. They were shepherds too, which accords with the account of Herodotus. * * * But having formed the opinion on grounds sufficiently assured, that the strangers who visited Egypt and superintended the building of the great pyramid were kinsmen of the patriarch Abraham, it is not very difficult to decide what was the subject respecting which they had such exact information. They or their parents had come from the land of the Chaldeans, and they were doubtless learned in all the wisdom of their Chaldean kinsmen. They were masters, in fact, of the astronomy of their day, a science for which the Chaldeans had shown, from the earliest ages, the most remarkable aptitude. * * * It is highly probable that the astronomical knowledge of the Chaldeans in the days of Terah and Abraham was much more accurate than that possessed by the Greeks in the time of Hipparchus." Mr. Proctor ultimately comes to the conclusion that "the stranger called Philition by Herodotus, may, for aught that appears, have been Abraham himself." It is a matter of secondary moment, in this consideration, whether Abraham himself or some other divinely inspired man, was the actual) architect of the great pyramid; it is sufficient to know, which it itself testifies, that whoever that builder was, he was acquainted with the same grand astronomical truths that the Book of Abraham states the Lord revealed to that patriarch, and which, at the time Joseph Smith translated the papyrus, were unknown to modern scientists.

Our next inquiries are, with regard to the causes or reasons that led to the erection of the pyramids, and to the purposes for which they were used.

Various theories have been advanced on these points. Some have supposed that these vast structures were associated with the religious rites of the ancient Egyptians; others have suggested that they combined the purposes of tombs and temples; again, that they were astronomical observatories; also that they had primarily astrological import. It has also been argued that they were defences against the sands of the great desert, or places of refuge during the excessive overflows of the Nile; the idea has also been advanced that they were granaries, somewhat after the manner of those erected under the direction of Joseph, the Israelite. A very little reflection will manifest that some of the suggestions are entirely untenable. Take for instance the notion that they were granaries. If so, what a vast waste of material, how entirely does their structure and form unsuit them for such a purpose. As wise a people as their builders must have been would scarcely have constructed a mountain of masonry, with two or three relatively small rooms therein, for such a purpose. There is some show of reason for believing that some of them were tombs and temples combined, but this will not hold good with regard to the pyramid of Cheops. Nothing found therein has given the least ground-work for the supposition that it was used for sepulchral purposes. In what is called the king's chamber was found an empty stone chest or coffer, without a lid; but in form, ornament and material it is entirely different to the usual sarcophagus used by the ancient Egyptians for the reception of the embalmed dead.

Two of the reasons advanced above, as applied to the pyramids of Cheops, are worthy of our consideration.

1st. That it was an astronomical observatory.

2d. That it was associated with the religion of the ancient Egyptians.

The reasons for believing it to have been built as an observatory are cogent and numerous. There can be no doubt that in many respects it was intended by its builders to typify astronomical truths; evidence in proof of which will be hereafter adduced. It has been suggested that the granite coffer found in what is now called the king's chamber (simply that it may have a distinctive name) was filled, in whole or in part, as circumstances required, with water, and that the face of the heavens was reflected therein, through the slanting passages that pointed directly to the polar star. That this coffer was used as a receptacle for water is highly probable, from the fact that a well tapping the waters of the Nile is found in the pyramid.[25] In this inner chamber, surrounded by this vast mass of masonry, removed as far as possible from the atmospheric and electric perturbations existing on the earth's surface, it is argued that using the water in the coffer as a mirror, the most accurate observations could be taken that were then possible. This idea we deem untenable, as it appears to us that the inclines and angles in the passages would render such reflection next to impossible. According to certain Arabian historians "there were placed in the great pyramid divers celestial spheres and stars, and what they severally operate in their aspects, and the perfumes which are to be used to them, and the books which treat of these matters."

The evidences that it was an edifice erected for sacred purposes are not so strong as those that can be brought forward in favor of its

---

[25] The assertion that this well connected with the Nile, is denied by Prof. Smyth and other explorers.

astronomical uses. We incline to the opinion that it combined both purposes; but we are scarcely willing to admit that if it was a temple, it was erected by a believer in the faith that looked upon Osiris and associate deities as the true Gods. The style of this vast structure and the temples erected by the followers of that faith are the antipodes of each other. The perfect purity of the pyramid from every idolatrous ornament and reference as well as of all attempts to glorify the wealth, might or wisdom of its human builders, makes it differ entirely, generically and radically from all ordinary Egyptian temples, pictured from top to bottom with the praises of their false gods. Besides, it is asserted, as before shown that the man who built this pyramid shut up the temples, a very inconsistent act, if he were a worshiper at their shrines. We hold the opinion that if this pyramid was used for religious purposes at all, it was in connection with the doctrines taught by Abraham, and if the Lord permitted the patriarch to preach to the Egyptians that principle of the Gospel known to us as baptism for the dead, we can well imagine the use to which the coffer in the king's chamber was applied. Indeed, the idea that the coffer was a baptismal font has been suggested by more than one Gentile writer,[26] but if it were used especially in the ordinances for the salvation of those who had passed from this sphere of action the symbolism would be almost perfect; for we have here a font enshrined in the heart of an artificial mountain, that could be reached only through a straight, stony gate and by a long, narrow and mysterious passage. How accurately these typify the valley of the shadow of death, and the grave, and how perfect the imagery of going into the heart of this solid mountain to act for those who had been laid away in the sepulchre. There is one thing that greatly strengthens the idea that if its uses were religious, they were Abrahamic. It is that this very coffer is of the exact capacity of the ark of the covenant of Moses' day, also that an originally marked oft portion of the chamber in which the coffer stands is of the exact capacity of the brazen sea, or baptismal font, in Solomon's Temple. Surely there is something more than a mere coincidence in this.

We next desire to draw attention to some of the important truths relating to the earth and the heavens, revealed by God to Abraham (as stated in part in his book), of which the generality of mankind of that and every succeeding age have remained in ignorance, even to the day in which we live, but with which the builders of the great pyramid were evidently acquainted. Amongst these and kindred truths, as manifested in the

[26] Bryant, Faber, Goodsir and others.

construction of this vast artificial mountain, we may mention the law of planetary and solar motion, the distance of the earth from its centre--the sun, the exact size, shape and density of our terraquous globe, the precise length of its solar orbit, as also the value of the sacred cubit as the unit of measurement. Writing on this subject, in a recent number of the Juvenile Instructor, Elder Joseph L. Barfoot (Beth) remarks: "There has been a great deal of guess-work heretofore about the use of the great pyramid at Geezah. The prevailing opinion was that it had been intended for a tomb for one of the ancient kings of Egypt, Discoveries have recently been made which have led to the inference that it had far more important uses, in fact that it was an observatory, built upon mathematical principles, and designed to perpetuate, through all succeeding time, a correct knowledge of the heavens and the earth. * * * It is found that the measure by which the proportions of the great pyramid were determined is an exact proportional to the axis of the earth itself. This is a very important thing, for it is thus in harmony with natural standards of measure, such as used by Deity. This pyramid standard measure is called the sacred cubit, as it is found that the standard divinely recognized through Moses was the same as that of the pyramid. The sacred cubit was the pyramid cubit."

Now then, with this fact before our eyes, let us turn to the Book of Abraham. The explanation of Fig. 1, of the circular disc, reads thus: "Kolob, signifying the first creation, nearest to the celestial, or the residence of God. First in government, the last pertaining to the measurement of time. The measurement, according to celestial time; which celestial time signifies one day to a cubit. One day in Kolob is equal to a thousand years, according to the measurement of this earth, which is-called by the Egyptians Jah-oh-eh."

If we understand the above aright it means that with the Gods the unit of the measurement of time is one of the days of Kolob, or one thousand of our years, "which celestial time signifies one day to a cubit," or, that as one of Kolob's days is the unit of celestial time, so the cubit is the unit of celestial measurement, by which the size of the worlds are measured when the foundations thereof are laid; by which the distances of the suns and planets are regulated, and all the creations of the Holy Ones controlled. That this cubit, which was the unit of measurement of holy things on this earth--the ark of the tabernacle, the temple, etc., was also the unit of measurement when this earth was created, is further proven by the following extract from Elder Barfoot's writings: "The sacred cubit is in length rather more than twenty-five (25.025) inches of English measure. It is one ten-millionth part of the radius of the axis of the earth at the poles;" that is, it is 10,000,000 sacred cubits from the centre of the earth to either the north or south pole, or 20,000,000 through the earth from pole to pole. Brother Barfoot continues: "No higher or more reliable standard of extreme precision could be given to man than the measure of the polar radius, for all other terrestrial and celestial things relating to the earth are in proportion to this natural standard. So important are the discoveries made recently by means of the sacred cubit that men are surprised to think that the uses of the great pyramid have been so long concealed." To this remark of our esteemed brother we answer, the Lord had not turned the key; and here we pause for a moment to ask, and ask of all the world, how could Joseph Smith have possibly become acquainted with this great truth if God had not revealed it unto him. This one truth alone of which all the world was ignorant, of itself, in its revelation by him, proves him to have been a prophet of the Most High God.

We now turn to some of the peculiarities of the great pyramid, to which passing reference has before been made, gleaning our information from the writings of Petrie, Osborn, Smyth, Mackay, and others. We would observe, however, that our space prevents us from giving any but the more prominent references.

1st. For parts cosmocally and symbolically significant, the metric standard of the great pyramid is the sacred cubit, exactly one ten-millionth of the earth's polar radius, the only natural standard of both unique and extreme precision; a standard of divine origination, primeval, and preserved in the least disturbed line of Abraham's family (the Arabs) to the present day. (Mr. Wm. Petrie.)

Does not this testimony almost word for word confirm the statements of the Book of Abraham?

2d. The direction of the strait entrance passage, inclining at 26° 20' into the north side of the pyramid, was such that at the reputed date of its establishment[27] this direction was that of the primeval pole star, then at

[27] B. C. 2170, or exactly 4000 years before 1830, the date of the organization of the Church of Jesus Cfhrist in this dispensation.

its lower culmination, while Alcyone[28] (the centre of, or governing planet which controls our solar system) then near the celestial equator, was at its upper culmination, or on the same meridian at midnight of the autumnal equinox. This definite combination cannot recur for 25,898 years; it marked the date of the pyramid, and of the year of the Pleiades," a commencement of a natural chronologic era, traditions of which have remained in most times and countries, or to put it in another shape, "the meridian of the primeval pole star became rigidly stationary on Alcyone at the date of the great pyramid, after which it commenced to retrograde."

3d. A thousand billion times the pyramid's weight, carefully computed, is the mass of the whole earth, namely, six thousand and fifty trillions of British tons.

4th. The annual circuit of the earth--that is, one year, is represented by the length of the base circuit of the pyramid, and each day of twenty-four hours by four cubits. Or each day of our year is represented by one cubit on each of the four sides of the pyramid, each side representing in its whole length one year of this earth. Or one day to a cubit as stated in the Book of Abraham. Can any one explain to us why this pyramid were so built that one cubit should represent one day exactly, if Abraham did not teach this to them? and if he did, then we have called the pyramids to bear witness to the truth of his book, which they most assuredly do, and at the same time to the truth of its translation by the Prophet Joseph Smith. Napoleon Bonaparte, when he gathered his armies in Egypt, pointing to the pyramids, told his legions that forty centuries looked down upon them. We have also called these mighty monuments of the past to bear record to the unity of revealed truth. Admit the above to be facts, and how is it possible to deny that Joseph Smith received his wisdom from a divine source, and consequently was a prophet of God.

Mr. Mackay, writing (1870) on facts in astronomy, states that the great pyramid has been "investigated and explored as no other monument,

---

[28] "The Pleiades are the seven stars, called cemah, which means an axle, that on or around which something turns. Now, a few years ago, Prof. Madler, the German astronomer, was awarded a gold medal by the scientific societies of Europe. And why? Because he was the first to advance the hypothesis of the existence of a central body in the stellar universe, about which all in our system revolved. He fixed, as that preponderating mass, upon the Pleiades, and upon the brightest star in the group, namely, Alcyone, as the very centre. Yet from Job we learn this scientific fact, and Prof. Madler had no special claim for such a discovery, nor had he any right to such a medal, unless he was a lineal descendant and heir of Job."--Dr. Wild, of New York.

ancient and modern, ever was; and the indefatigable explorers have been rewarded with an abundant harvest of the most brilliant discoveries. One of these, discovered by Mr. Petrie, is the clear indication that the architect of this pyramid knew the mean distance of the sun from the earth with an exactitude to which modern science never approached till within the last seven years. * * * The best lineal and angular measurements have been combined by W. Petrie, who shows therefrom that the original height of the great pyramid, from the pavement to its base, was 486.25 British feet; this multiplied by the ninth power of ten--i.e., 1,000,000,000 gives a result of 92,093,000 British miles, for the mean distance of the sun. The latest collective result of science reckons the probable truth to be between 91,970,000, and 92,150,000; while the great pyramid gives 92,093,000 miles,[29] being completely within these minimum uncertainties of science." This, by other references, has been proven to have been no accident, but intended by the builders, as it constitutes but a small part of the evidence discovered in this direction.

Here, then, we have evidence that the ancient Egyptians had a knowledge of the true distance from the sun. That they obtained this knowledge only by divine light is evidenced by the abortive attempts of other ancient investigators to determine this question. For instance, in the days of Herodotus, (B. C. 500,) it was thought that the sun was distant only some eight or ten miles; fifty years later it was estimated by Anaxagoras at 1800; 150 years later, 5,300,000 was the computed distance; 1900 years later, Kepler calculated the distance at 26,400,000 miles; in A. D. 1750 the supposed distance was increased to 81,650,000, and so, from the dawn of creation until now, uninspired men have been groping after this truth, and even to-day they are not entirely satisfied that the exact measurement has been obtained.

It is unnecessary, for our present purpose, to enter into all the details of the varied geometrical, metrical, mechanical, geographical, astronomical and cosmical references found in the great pyramid, all of which, it is vigorously asserted, have been tested and proven correct by the very best scientific ability; nor will space permit us to follow a rapidly-increasing class of writers who find in its lines, angles and markings a prophetic history of the world; but we should scarcely feel satisfied if we

---

[29] The most recent scientific estimate of the sun's distance from the earth actually places it within 270 miles of the exact pyramid figures.

did not summarize a few of its leading characteristics. "We find,"[30] to use the language of Dr. J. A. Seiss, of Philadelphia," a perfect geometric figure, so framed that the four sides of its base bear the same proportion to its vertical height as the circumference of a circle to its radius; that each of its base lines measures the even ten-millionth part of the semi-axis of the earth just as many times as there are days in the year; that its height multiplied by the ninth power of ten gives the mean distance between the earth and its great centre of light; that its unit of length is the even five hundredth millionth part of the polar diameter of the globe we inhabit; that its two diagonals of base measure in inches the precise number of years in the great processional cycle; that its bulk of masonry is an even proportion of the weight of the earth itself, and that its setting and shaping are squared and oriented[31] with microscopic accuracy." Regarding the coffer in the king's chamber he continues: "We perceive in it a most accurately-shaped standard of measures and proportions, its sides and bottom cubically identical with its internal space, the length of its two sides to its height as a circle to its diameter, its exterior volume just twice the dimension of its bottom, and its whole measure just the fiftieth part of the chamber in which it was put when the edifice was built," for it could not have been gotten into the chamber after the building was finished, by reason of the size and angles of the entrance passages. Now, then, let us add to these facts a statement by the same author, and we think our position regarding the veracity of the portion of the Book of Abraham we have lastly been commenting upon is amply vindicated. "Everywhere do we encounter the traditions of Abraham's skill in the knowledge of the heavens, how he argued from his observation of the heavenly orbs, and how he occupied himself in Egypt teaching the priests of Heliopolis in the lore of the skies. Doubtless this was not the naked science of astronomy as the schools conceive of it, but as respected the theological and Messianic truths symbolized in these celestial hieroglyphics, in which, as in the more literal promises, he rejoiced to see Christ's day, and saw it and was glad. (John, viii, 56.)" Which testimony of the Savior's is in direct accord with the statements of the Book of Abraham; nor need we be surprised thereat, when revelation, ancient and modern, states that Enoch, and indeed other antediluvian patriarchs, saw not only "Christ's day," but the world's history, even to the winding up scene.

---

30 Miracle in Stone.

31 Oriented--situated with respect to the four cardinal points.

Admitting that the shape of the pyramid, in connection with its other references, has a prophetic import, it becomes a remarkable fact that this stupendous four-sided monument, in this particular phase of its construction, typifies the number of days, according to the reckoning of the Lord and of Kolob, between the fall of man and the incarnation of our Savior (4000 years), and the time between the date of its own construction and the organization of the Church of Jesus Christ in the last days (also 4000 years), Two of the most important events then in the future of the world's history, and known in the economy of God, the first as the ushering in of "the dispensation of the fulness of time," the second as the ushering in of "the dispensation of the fulness of times."

CHAPTER 9

SCIENTIFIC OBJECTIONS TO THE PROPHET'S TRANSLATION OF THE BOOK OF ABRAHAM.--F. DEVERIA'S TRANSLATION.--SAMPLES OF ANCIENT LANGUAGES IN THE BOOK OF ABRAHAM.--WORD ROOTS.--LACK OF CHRONOLOGIC SEQUENCE.--CONCLUSION.

IN the year 1855, Messrs. Remy and Brenchly, two French travelers, visited Utah. On their return to Paris they carried with them a copy of the Book of Abraham, which they placed in the hands of "a young savant of the Museum of the Louvre, M. Theodule Deveria," with the request that he would translate it. This he attempted to do. Messrs. Remy and Brenchly afterwards published an account of their travels, and embodied therein M. Deveria's soi-disant translation. They pretend to consider that the disclosures made by the scientific translation should place the Book of Abraham in the catalogue of the pious frauds that have so often disgraced the history of religion. We come to an entirely opposite conclusion, and claim that so far as M. Deveria's translation is concerned, if it does anything, it substantiates the statements of the Prophet Joseph with regard to the true meaning of the papyri. Two things, however, have to be remembered--the first, that the Egyptian hieroglyphics had at least two (but more probably three) meanings, the one understood by the masses--the other comprehended only by the initiated, the priesthood and others; which latter conveyed the true though hidden intent of the writer. The second consideration is that when M, Deveria made his translation, Egyptiology, as a science, was in its babyhood. Since then highly important discoveries have been made in this branch of literature, which have greatly changed the con. elusions of earlier students. But even to-day the science is so inexact that but a few weeks ago the Deseret News published an anecdote of two eminent Egyptiologists, who unitedly came to the conclusion that the hieroglyphics on the wrappings of a mummy they were examining proved the deceased to have been a great warrior or king among the ancient Egyptians. On removing the inner bandages, the body proved to be that of a woman. If the scientists of today make such egregious blunders, what may we expect from Messrs. Remy and Brenchly's young savant of twenty years ago, before Osborn, Smyth, and others, had made the important discoveries that are almost revolutionizing the ideas of the learned on ancient Egypt and its literature.

We will now draw attention to a few of the differences between the two translations.

The Prophet Joseph Smith states that Plate I represents an idolatrous priest attempting to offer up Abraham as a sacrifice to his gods. M. D. affirms that it represents the resurrection of Osiris. We ask, if it is a representation of a resurrection, what is the priest doing with a knife in his hand? Osiris was not resurrected with a knife, but Abraham would have been slain with one if God had not delivered him. And it is a somewhat remarkable fact that the original Egyptian hieroglyphic for the verb Nohem, to rescue, to deliver, was a bedstead-shaped altar with a bird flying above it, just as represented in Plate I, of the angel of the Lord rescuing Abraham. Is it not probable that the hieroglyphic had its origin in this very circumstance?

Joseph the Prophet says Fig. 1 represents "the angel of the Lord." M. D. states that it is "the soul of Osiris under the form of a hawk (which should have a human head)." Fig. 3, the Prophet states, is "the idolatrous priest of Elkenah." M. D. says it is "the god Anubis (who should have a jackal's head)," and in other places he makes substantially the same statement, that a certain figure represents somebody or something, or would do so if it were different. This puts us in mind of a little story. A certain clergyman was visiting the home of one of his parishoners, when he noticed a little son of his host very busily engaged, first intently eyeing him and then working away at a slate he held in his hand. Suspecting what he was doing, the clergyman asked the boy if he was not drawing his portrait, and finding his suspicions were correct, he asked to see it. With some reluctance the boy consented. After looking at it a moment, the clergyman exclaimed: "Why, this is not like me!" and received in reply the very consoling answer, "Well, I guess it's not; suppose I put a tail on it and call it a dog." So M. Deveria wants to put a head or a tail on some of these characters and then call them Osiris, Anubis, or some other God! Anything to beat revelation.

In a great many instances, though the wording in the inspired translation varies greatly from the scientific attempt, yet the idea is almost identical. Placed together, they substantiate the statement of an eminent modern writer on Egyptian literature, who declares that at first sight the religious branch of this literature "seems to proclaim the Egyptians the most polytheistic of men, but a more careful examination leads to the supposition that the various gods were only intended to bring out in symbol and in allegory the various qualities and manifestations of one great God, incarnate, eternal and omnipotent." Joseph's translation conveying the higher though hidden meaning, and M. D. the presumedly literal intent of the hieroglyphics. For instance, Pig. 9, Plate I, is stated by the prophet to represent "the idolatrous god of Pharaoh;" M. D. calls it "the sacred crocodile, symbolic of the god Sebat." Sebat was certainly a god to Pharaoh, so wherein lies the difference? Again, Fig. 3, Plate II, "is made to represent God sitting upon his throne, clothed with power and authority, with a crown of eternal light upon his head." The scientist says it is "the god Ra, the sun, with a hawk's head, seated in his boat." What great difference is there in the idea? and how did Joseph Smith know that it represented God (call him by what typical name you like) if not by revelation ? What is there in the figure of a cow (Fig. 6) to convey the idea to an unlearned man that it had reference to the hosts of heaven? yet both translations distinctly convey that idea. Figs. 12 to 20 (Plate II), Joseph says will be given in the own due time of the Lord. M, D. does not attempt to translate them, he says they are "illegibly copied," "cannot be deciphered," "illegible in the copy," etc., and so gets out of the difficulty, but not without insinuating that the MSS. have been "intentionally altered." But what earthly reason there could be for the "Mormons" attempting to alter them, is beyond our comprehension. At any rate he does not translate them. . As a sample of how M. D. twists definitions on purpose to give a different translation from that of the prophet, we have an instance in Plate I, in the figures representing the gods of Elkenah, Libnah, Mahmackrah and Korash, which our French savant states represent the Canopian vessels or jars. And what are the Canopian jars? Certain jars first found at Canopus, a city at the mouth of the Nile, and because the learned did not, nor do not now know, with certainty, their intent,[32] they called them after the place where they were found. But because they were found at Canopus is it any reason that they should net be the gods Joseph Smith represents them to be ? The learned believe them to be gods, but their researches result in no definite conclusions. The Prophet Joseph associates them with the god of the ruler of Egypt, which statement placed along side of the fact that they were found in Egypt, gives strength and consistency to his translation. M. D.'s translation is simply begging the question so far as attempting to prove the inaccuracy of Joseph's translation is concerned.

---

[32] See article "Canopus," in American Cyclopaedia.

Exceptions are taken by M. Deveria to some of the proper names that appear in the Book of Abraham, and which our martyred prophet informs us were Egyptian. Messrs. Remy and Brenchly apply the word "gibberish" to certain portions of the book, which we suppose must relate to such words, as the English portion is plain enough and gibberish means senseless or unmeaning talk or gabble. To enter into a detailed account of the root of each Egyptian or Chaldean word given in the book would be very tedious to the most of our readers; we shall therefore simply summarize by saying, that so far as we have been able to trace through the authorities at our disposal, which are very meagre, three things are evident:

1st. That the words given by Joseph have true roots.

2d. That these roots are from the languages of the countries known to Abraham.

3d. That the meanings of these roots are consistent with the meanings of the words as translated by Joseph Smith.

All of which proves that they are not gibberish.

As an instance of how far M. D. goes out of his way to attack these words, he remarks on the statement of Abraham that this earth was by the Egyptians called Jah-oh-eh; that "the word Jah-oh-eh has nothing Egyptian in it, it resembles the Hebrew word Jehovah badly translated." If it has nothing Egyptian in it how does it happen that the word Jehovah itself has been claimed by many to be an Egyptian and not a Hebrew word? With regard to which see Dr. Smith's Dictionary of the Bible. It is also positive that this sacred word was known to other nations as well as the covenant people of God, as it is to be found, in its exact form, and applied to the God of the Hebrews, on line eighteen of the Moabite stone, lately translated by Sir Henry Rawlinson.

There are other words that are objected to as not being Egyptian. In reply we ask, How can M. Deveria or any one else, at the present stage of Egyptiology, tell whether a word was Egyptian or not? Joseph has undoubtedly written the word in the English characters that best represented the actual sound of the word in ancient Egyptian. Scientists know nothing positive of those sounds; they knew that certain hieroglyphics form certain words with certain supposed meaning, but for the sounds they have to rely on the language of the modern Copts, basing their theory on the slender foundation that the sounds of words in Egypt are the same to-day as they were 4000 years ago. We well know that customs, habits, etc., change but little in the stagnant lives of the inhabitants of Egypt, Canaan, and kindred nations, but it is almost too great a stretch on our credulity to ask us to accept as definite the assumed sound of a word in Abraham's day, because it is pronounced in that way now. For instance, who can, with certainty, assert how the ancient Egyptians pronounced the name of their own country? Was it Kham-to, or Gyp-to, or Egyptos, or indeed Ghubsi?

There are certainly some words in the record that are evidently Egyptian. Such as Kli-flos-is-es, the name of one of the stars. All Egyptiologists admit that Isis relates to the moon. But it may be urged that Joseph Smith obtained these words from some Egyptian work. Not so; for the first grammar and dictionary of ancient Egyptian published in modern times (between 1836 and 1844)--those of M. Champollion-- were not published until after the translation of the papyrus by the Prophet Joseph. So that objection falls to the ground.

In the word Kolob we have another instance of a word whose roots are to be frequently found in the languages of Phoenicia and the neighboring nations, and the word[33] itself appears in the languages of some of the descendants of Abraham (certain tribes of the American Indians) at the present time. But probably this is enough on the subject of language.

There are two other points to which we win allude, that are strong internal evidence of the genuineness of the Book of Abraham. One is, that in its historical portion no reference, however slight, is made to events that occurred after its assumed date of composition. Had Joseph Smith been its author, the probabilities are strongly in favor of circumstances being mentioned therein that did not take place until after the time that the book claims to have been written. Had Joseph been a man well versed in the history of the world in Abraham's day, the probabilities would not have been so great; but ignorant as he was, so far as book learning is concerned, of ancient history, this simple circumstance alone is strong evidence in favor of its authenticity.

---

[33] Kolob signifies in their language the eye (or light) of the world.

The other point to which we wish to draw attention is the lack of chronological sequence in the historical portions of the book, a trait manifested in the writings of many of the patriarch's descendants, and which we believe to have been general with the writers living in the early age of the world. Chronologic accuracy, in the writers of personal or historical narratives, appears to have been the outgrowth of a later age.

The concluding portions of the Book of Abraham are mainly historical, and relate to circumstances that occurred in the heavens in man's pre-existent state, and at the creation of the world. These subjects have been so ably handled by others that we shall not attempt to treat upon them here. Besides, they are somewhat foreign to our subject, and directly have no bearing on the truth of the Abrahamic record, having been made plain in other revelations of God's word. We shall therefore, with this chapter, conclude our review of the Book of Abraham, but before doing so must acknowledge the aid we have received from many wise suggestions and valuable information afforded us by President John Taylor, Elders Franklin D. Richards, Joseph L. Barfoot, John R. Howard, David McKenzie and others.

In conclusion we would say, that we believe that those who have carefully followed us through this inquiry must be satisfied that the Abrahamic record is genuine. We have appealed to ancient historians and modern scientists, and they have not failed us; we have called to our aid the monuments of ancient Egypt, and they have borne unequivocal testimony; we have examined the glorious system of astronomy advanced in its pages, and find it is being substantiated by modern research; internally we have found its unities well preserved, nor have we discovered a contradiction within its pages. As with the Book of Mormon, so with the Book of Abraham, we feel fully assured, that every day as it passes, every new discovery that has a bearing on its statements, will increasingly vindicate its truthfulness, and bear united testimony that Joseph Smith Was indeed and of a truth a Prophet, Seer and Revelator, inspired by the Spirit of Jehovah, the mighty god of Jacob.

www.ingramcontent.com/pod-product-compliance
Lightning Source LLC
LaVergne TN
LVHW050944080826
845145LV00004B/1398